TO:

FROM:

DATE:

faithgirlz

Fearless Faith

100 DEVOTIONS FOR GIRLS

Melanie Shankle

ZONDER**kidz**

To my sweet Caroline:

May you always have the kind of faith
that makes you fearless. Be brave, be kind,
be all that God made you to be.

Introduction

I have a daughter who's just a little bit older than you probably are right now, but I have watched her learn to trust God in so many ways over the last few years. I remember being your age and trying to figure out what God wanted me to do with my life and how I could make a difference in the world around me. The bottom line is we are living in a time that calls for fearless faith.

It won't always be easy to do the right thing or to stand up for what you believe in because there will be people around you who won't understand. But we serve a God who has called us to things bigger than we can even imagine, and he is with us every step of the way. We all have times when we feel afraid, when it's hard to trust God to help us get through all the challenges that come our way. But fearless faith helps us do what he is calling us to in spite of feeling afraid. My hope is that the devotions and activities in this book will help you know God more and remind you that he has made you kind, fierce, and brave. The world is waiting for you, sweet girl, to shine bright.

Love,

Melanie

DAY 1

Have I not commanded you? Be strong
and courageous. Do not be afraid; do not
be discouraged, for the LORD your God
will be with you wherever you go.

JOSHUA 1: 9

Every single one of us is afraid of something. Even those of us who seem to be brave are usually just better than others at hiding how scared we really are. But you know what's amazing? That God knows how scared we feel and uses us for his purposes anyway.

I once read that the phrase "Do not fear" or "Fear not" is used 365 times throughout the Bible. There will be very few times in our lives when there isn't some situation to be afraid of. In *The Wizard of Oz*, the cowardly Lion spends his whole journey searching for courage and when he finally meets the Great Wizard of Oz, he is told that true courage is facing danger even when you're afraid.

No doubt Joshua was terrified as the time grew near for him to lead the people of Israel across the Jordan River and into the Promised Land. But God assured him in Joshua 1:5 that "No one will be able to stand against you all the days of your life. As I was with Moses, so I will be with you; I will never leave you nor forsake you." And God promises us the same.

TAKEAWAY

Fearful times will come, scary circumstances will arise, giants will stand in our way, but we have a God who is with us always, whispering that true courage is when we walk ahead in our fear and take the leap of faith, always knowing that he promises to never leave us.

WRITE ABOUT IT...

What scares you? How can you be fearless instead of afraid?

DAY 2

For we are God's handiwork, created in
Christ Jesus to do good works, which
God prepared in advance for us to do.

EPHESIANS 2:10

Sometimes it's easy to look around and wish we were more like someone else. We wish we could sing like this person or make really good grades like one of our friends always does. Or maybe we wish we had long, blonde hair or that we didn't have so many freckles across our nose. Maybe there has even been a time when someone said hurtful things about us that make us feel like we aren't good enough or smart enough.

But Psalm 139 says that we are wonderfully and fearfully made. He created each one of us very specifically to live in this time and in this generation, just the way we are. Our school, our friends, and our family wouldn't be the same without the unique way we have been created. Psalm 17:8 says we are the apple of God's eye. Psalm 18:19 says, "He rescued me because he delights in me." Isaiah 49:16 says, "He has engraved me on the palms of his hands." Zephaniah 3:17 says, "He takes great delight in me. He will quiet me with his love and rejoice over me with singing."

That is some serious love. That is a God that wants to give us hope and a future. That is a God who sees us as his masterpiece.

 TAKEAWAY

God made each one of us with specific plans and purposes in mind. He gave us talents, gifts, and abilities that are unique to us. It's our job to find out what those are and use them well.

 WRITE ABOUT IT...

What are some of your gifts?

_____

_____

_____

_____

_____

_____

DAY 3

. . . we will not compare ourselves with each
other as if one of us were better and another
worse. We have far more interesting things to
do with our lives. Each of us is an original.

GALATIANS 5:26 (THE MESSAGE)

We all love Instagram and Snapchat, but at the same time, we have never had so many ways to compare our lives to our friends' lives. We know what they are eating for breakfast, if they're having a party, or when they are on vacation.

It can look like everyone's life is better than ours. There's a famous quote that says, "Comparison is the thief of joy" because when you pay too much attention to what someone else has, it's easy to forget all the good things God has given you.

We need to remember that social media isn't real. It's a quick, beautiful picture that may not even be as great as it looks on Snapchat. We all have our own unique gifts. Life is too short for comparison. We need to walk our own road and not spend our time looking to the left and the right to see what everyone else is doing.

Let's encourage each other to be the best version of who God has called us to be and cheer each other on. That's how you build a solid foundation for real friendship. And remember, God has far more interesting things for each of us to do with our lives than spend our time comparing it to someone else.

TAKEAWAY

You are an original.

WRITE ABOUT IT . . .

Instead of comparing yourself to someone else, list five things you like most about yourself.

_____

_____

_____

_____

_____

Am I now trying to win the approval of
men or of God? Or am I trying to please
men? If I were still trying to please men,
I would not be a servant of Christ.

GALATIANS 1:10

Many of us are people pleasers. We want everyone to like us. We want everyone to think we're a nice person. We like to just blend into a crowd and not open ourselves up in a way that may cause people to say, "Well, that's weird."

We live in a world where approval matters. So much of what we post online is about wanting to get likes or have people tell us how great or funny we are.

The problem is, there will always be people who don't like us, sometimes for reasons we don't understand. Which is why we need to remind ourselves that the only approval that matters comes from God. Nobody knows you like God knows you. And since only God knows us inside out, his approval is the one that matters.

What will help you overcome the fear of what others think about you is asking God to help you find true security that can only come from Him, which means knowing who you are in Christ, what he has done for you, and that you are so dearly loved.

TAKEAWAY

Find the thing and purpose for which you were created and quit worrying what others will think of you. When we are doing what God created us to do, we will find much happiness in that, and we won't care as much what other people think.

WRITE ABOUT IT ...

Use the journaling lines below to list the things you love to do the most.

DAY 5

When I consider your heavens, the work of your
fingers, the moon and the stars, which you have
set in place, what is mankind that you are mindful
of them, human beings that you care for them?

PSALM 8: 3–4

Every night the entire sky is full of stars that shine bright even when we can't see them. Our God placed each of those stars in the universe. There are too many to count—stars that have yet to be discovered, stars that have shone for millions of years, and stars whose light burned out long ago. Yet God knows them all because he put them there. He is so vast, so powerful. He holds every single bit of the universe in his hands.

And he chose us. He could have stuck to creating stars. You have to believe they'd give him a lot less trouble than we do sometimes. But he created all these things and then he created us. Not because he had to, but because of love.

TAKEAWAY

Just like God holds all those stars in the night sky, he holds every detail of our lives in his hands.

WRITE ABOUT IT . . .

What do you think God wants for your life?

_____

_____

_____

_____

_____

_____

_____

DAY 6 • ACTIVITY #1:
VISION BOARD

>>>>>>—∞·—·—·—·∞·—→

Make a vision board with your goals, dreams, and hopes
for the future. Add your favorite Bible verses about who
God says you are and hang it in your room to remind
you of all the things that are important to you.

How to make a vision board:

- Use a whiteboard, corkboard, or piece of poster board, depending on your style.
- Write down what you love, what makes you happy, what your dreams are for the future. You can use markers, glitter, stickers, and pages that you cut out of magazines.
- Post photos of your favorite moments (winning the soccer game, performing at a recital, meeting your favorite author).
- Write down Bible verses that inspire you.
- Make a list of goals you want to accomplish in the next sports season, school year, or even by the time you finish middle school or high school.

DAY 7

God hasn't given us a spirit of fear but of power and of love and of sound mind.

2 TIMOTHY 1:7

Have you ever laid in bed at night and felt afraid of the dark? Do you let your imagination run away with you until you forget the truth—that God is bigger than all our fears? Do you worry that something might happen to you, someone in your family, or a friend? God never wants us to feel afraid which is why he gives us a spirit of power and of love and sound mind.

When we start to feel those crazy, scary thoughts, we can fight them with a sound mind and God's power. There are some great Bible verses to memorize about how fear has no place in our lives and has no power over us (check out Joshua 1:9 or Psalm 23:4). Repeat those silently in your head to help reject any fear you are feeling and remind yourself that God loves you and that you are never alone.

We can spend our whole lives worrying about scary things and miss out on what God has in store for us because we are so focused on all the things that make us feel afraid. Or we can learn to trust him with our fears and ask him to fill our minds with the truth of his love and protection.

TAKEAWAY

When we trust God with our fears, he will help us feel less afraid.

WRITE ABOUT IT . . .

Write down the top five things that scare you. Then ask God to help you overcome those fears.

DAY 8

For you formed my inward parts; you knitted me
together in my mother's womb. I praise you, for
I am fearfully and wonderfully made. Wonderful
are your works; my soul knows it very well.

PSALM 139:13–14 (ESV)

Have you ever looked at pictures of your mom or dad when they were little and realized how much you look like them? It's amazing how God knits us together in a way that we are completely unique, but can still have our mom's smile or our dad's eyes.

It makes me think of Psalm 139 where David writes that he is "fearfully and wonderfully made." When you look at the original Hebrew words the Bible was written in, fearfully means "with heartfelt interest" and the word wonderfully means "unique and set apart." It makes us realize how much love and thought went into our design as God created each one of us. We are his masterpieces.

And if we let that really sink in, we can understand just a little bit how much he loves and cares for us. None of us are here by accident. We were knit together with great love by our creator. He could have made anything, but he chose to make you with all your quirks and freckles and personality.

TAKEAWAY

When hard times come, we may be tempted to wonder if God cares. Of course he does. He's the one who knit us together from the beginning and continues to hold all the pieces of our life in his hands.

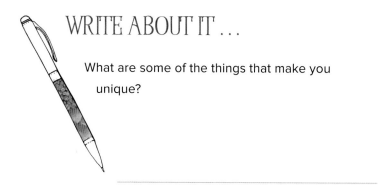

WRITE ABOUT IT ...

What are some of the things that make you unique?

DAY 9

"My grace is sufficient for you, for my power
is made perfect in weakness." Therefore, I will
boast all the more gladly about my weaknesses,
so that Christ's power may rest on me.

2 CORINTHIANS 12:9

One thing the Bible reminds us of over and over again is that we don't need to be perfect. We are loved by God no matter how many times we mess up or how weak we may be at times. The truth is his grace is bigger than all our failures.

But we know ourselves. We know what we've done and how we've messed up. And we can feel so disappointed in ourselves that we assume God must be disappointed too. How does he look at us with love and hope that we'll do better tomorrow, but won't love us any less if we don't?

It doesn't make sense.

We are hardest on ourselves. We get caught up in the comparison game and feel like everyone is doing better than us. But God has never once looked at you, shook his head, and said, "Wow. What a failure. I should have gotten someone else to do that." That's not how he works.

I don't know if any of us can ever fully grasp the love of God. It's too big. And maybe we aren't meant to understand, but just to sink deeper into his grace and love for us.

TAKEAWAY

God's love for us is bigger than any mistake we have made.

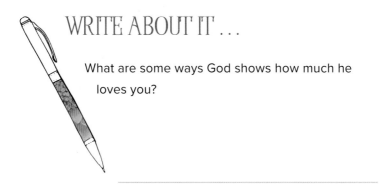

WRITE ABOUT IT ...

What are some ways God shows how much he loves you?

The Lord will fight for you; you need only to be still.

EXODUS 14:14

Have you ever seen a little bird fight its own reflection in the window? They puff up their feathers and peck at the glass because they think they are actually fighting another bird when the truth is, there is nothing there to fight. It's a battle they made up in their own head.

We all have times in our life when we feel threatened and afraid. Maybe someone has hurt our family, maybe we've been let down by someone we trusted, maybe the world just seems like a scary place. And our instinct in these times is to fight. We fight to protect the ones we love and ourselves. Surely we can't just stand around and let bad things happen. We have to come out swinging.

But sometimes our fighting is as silly and pointless as the little bird who fights his own reflection. We don't even know what we're fighting against or who the real enemy is, and so we just peck and flutter around in a frenzy without accomplishing much of anything other than wearing ourselves out.

Meanwhile, we have a God who promises to fight for us. He sees the entire picture while we see what we *think* is the problem. The best thing we can do is call on him to fight our battles and learn to trust that he is working all things together for our good. He is our defender, our strong tower, our mighty God.

TAKEAWAY

God fights our battles for us. We just need to rest in his promises and remember that he is on our side.

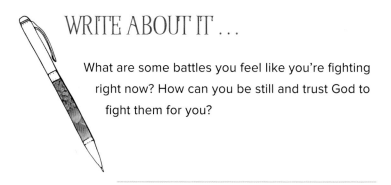

WRITE ABOUT IT . . .

What are some battles you feel like you're fighting right now? How can you be still and trust God to fight them for you?

DAY 11

> By faith Moses' parents hid him for three
> months after he was born, because they
> saw he was no ordinary child, and they
> were not afraid of the king's edict.
>
> HEBREWS 11:23

Jochebed was the mother of Moses. She gave birth to him at a time when Pharaoh had ordered that all Hebrew baby boys under the age of three be killed. But Jochebed saw something in her baby, Moses, that led her to know that he wasn't an ordinary child. And so, by faith, she and her husband hid Moses for three months despite the orders from Pharaoh.

But the day finally came when she knew she couldn't hide him anymore. She had to do something even more difficult; she had to let her baby go and trust God with the rest. Jochebed put Moses in a basket and set him in the Nile River. She had to believe that God was going to take care of one of the things she loved most in the world.

Moses ended up being raised in the most powerful household in all of Egypt, which paved the way for him to be the one God used to lead the Hebrews out of slavery and captivity. The faithfulness of Jochebed set in a motion a plan that changed the pages of history.

We've all had to accept answers to prayers that didn't turn out the way we wanted, but Jochebed's story is a reminder that God is always working out better things for us than anything we could imagine.

TAKEAWAY

There will be times when it feels like God is asking us to give up something we love, but we can trust that he will use it for good and give us something better in return.

WRITE ABOUT IT …

Is there anything you feel God is asking you to give to him right now?

DAY 12 • ACTIVITY #2:
BIBLE VERSE INSPIRATION

Here are some great verses to get you started:

Isaiah 42:16   Psalm 118:24
Psalm 27:1   Romans 8:28
Proverbs 3:5–6

1. Find some note cards or other pretty paper and your favorite markers or pens.

2. Write down some of your favorite Bible verses that encourage you or remind you to have fearless faith.

3. Use artwork and stickers to make them pretty and colorful.

4. Tape up these cards where you will see them every day . . . in your bathroom while you're brushing your teeth, in your bedroom, or even in your school locker or lunchbox.

DAY 13

Now Israel loved Joseph more than any of his
other sons, because he had been born to him
in his old age; and he made an ornate robe for
him. When his brothers saw that their father
loved him more than any of them, they hated
him and could not speak a kind word to him.

GENESIS 37: 3–4

When we read the story of Joseph, we learn that Joseph's
family was complicated. His father, Jacob, stole the
birthright from his brother with the help of his mother and
then had to run away. Jacob worked for his uncle, Laban,
so he could marry Rachel, the woman he loved, only to be
tricked into marrying her sister, Leah. Rachel couldn't have
children for a long time but Leah gave birth to many sons.
Finally, when Rachel gave birth to Joseph, he became Jacob's
favorite son. Jacob made him a coat of many colors but his
brothers were jealous of him and it was only made worse when
Joseph told them he had a dream in which they all bowed
down to him. His brothers wanted to kill him, but instead
they threw him in a pit and sold him into slavery.

Joseph's story ends with the realization that God used every
part of his story, even his brothers' hatred, for a bigger purpose. God took all that hurt and jealousy and turned it
around for good.

He can do the same for us. If we trust God enough, we can let go of the ways someone has hurt us. We can even ask him to help us use that hard time to learn something important.

TAKEAWAY

There may be times when a friend or family member hurts your feelings or isn't kind to you. God can use that hurt to help you make a difference in your life or the life of someone you love.

WRITE ABOUT IT . . .

Was there ever a time someone really hurt you but you were able to forgive them? Did it make you feel better to forgive that person?

DAY 14

Take your everyday, ordinary life—your sleeping,
eating, going-to-work, and walking-around
life—and place it before God as an offering.
Embracing what God does for you is the best
thing you can do for him. Don't become so
well-adjusted to your culture that you fit into it
without even thinking. Instead, fix your attention
on God. You'll be changed from the inside out.

ROMANS 12:1–2 (THE MESSAGE)

There are times when life can seem kind of boring. Every
day, day after day seems exactly the same. And maybe
you look around and it feels like other peoples' lives are a lot
more interesting.

But God has put you exactly where you are for a reason and a
purpose. Only you and your unique personality can affect the
people around you every day in your own special way. God
takes all of what you do—the exciting and the boring and the
ordinary parts of your life—and makes it something special.

No one else can live your story. Your life is a work of art, and
God is the artist, using you and your experiences to paint
the world. So embrace all that is unique about your life and
realize that is exactly what makes it special. Don't try so hard
to fit in. That's how you'll change the world.

 TAKEAWAY

You are uniquely and purposefully made for your life.

WRITE ABOUT IT...

What are some things that make you different from other people around you? How can you use those things to make a difference to other people?

_____

_____

_____

_____

_____

_____

DAY 15

Gracious words are a honeycomb, sweet
to the soul and healing to the bones.

PROVERBS 16:24

Have you ever tasted honeycomb? Not just honey, but the actual honeycomb? It is so sweet and delicious. And best of all, honey is actually good for you. It can make your allergies better and even help your body heal itself when you're sick and fighting a cold. Maybe that's why this verse compares our kind words to honeycomb. The words we speak to others can help heal their hurts or just come at a time when someone really needs some kindness. Our words can be life to another person.

Just because someone doesn't look you in the eye and say, "Hey, you know what? I really need you to say something nice to me right now," doesn't mean that they don't need to hear positive, loving words. Sometimes the best thing we can do is take the time to tell someone that they matter, they are appreciated, and to fill them up with a little bit of kindness.

TAKEAWAY

God uses us to make a difference when we show his love to our friends through the words we speak.

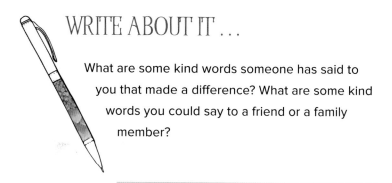

WRITE ABOUT IT . . .

What are some kind words someone has said to you that made a difference? What are some kind words you could say to a friend or a family member?

> But a Samaritan, as he traveled, came where
> the man was; and when he saw him, he took
> pity on him. He went to him and bandaged
> his wounds, pouring on oil and wine. Then
> he put the man on his own donkey, took
> him to an inn and took care of him.
>
> LUKE 10:33–34

When Jesus tells the story of the good Samaritan, he talks about a man who had been robbed, beaten, and left for dead. A priest and a Levite, who were both considered holy men of that time, passed him by and ignored his pain. But it was a Samaritan, a person considered a social outcast, that took pity on the man. The Samaritan not only took care of the man in that moment, but left money for the innkeeper and asked him to look after him until he was well. Jesus says the Samaritan was the man who was the neighbor.

We all have both big and small ways that we can be a good neighbor, in so many areas of our life. It can be as simple as getting the mail for an older person who lives down the street or welcoming the new kid at school. Or you can volunteer at a soup kitchen or help on a mission trip at your church. Your neighbors aren't just the people next door—they are people all over the world!

God has placed us in unique areas of our world where he calls us to be his hands and feet. To love the hurting, to take care of the sick, and to carry each other's burdens when we can't carry them alone. Where can we help? Where can we make a difference? Where can we be a good Samaritan?

TAKEAWAY

God uses us to help those around us.

WRITE ABOUT IT . . .

What are some ways you can help someone in need? How can you be kind to someone around you?

DAY 17

In the same way, let your light shine before
others, that they may see your good deeds
and glorify your Father in heaven.

MATTHEW 5:16

Have you ever tried to read a book and realized you were having a hard time seeing the words because there wasn't enough light in the room? Or have you ever been outside at night, in the middle of nowhere, and realized how much darker it is when there aren't any city lights shining into the sky?

It's amazing the difference that a little light can make. A place can look so frightening and unfamiliar in the dark. But once you shine a little bit of light, you suddenly realize that those scary things you thought you saw were just a chair or a coat hanging on the back of a closet door.

It's like that with the light of Jesus that shines in us. The world can seem so big and scary. We can start to feel like everything around us is dark because we forget about the light that lives inside of us. We can get used to that light over time and take it for granted. But with each person we meet, we have the power to make a big difference in their life just by letting our light shine. We have been given all the power of Christ to shine brightly in this world, and it's good to remember what a difference that light can bring to a dark place.

TAKEAWAY

We can let the light of Jesus shine bright in our lives through the words we speak and the way we live.

WRITE ABOUT IT . . .

How can you let your light shine? Is there a way you can be a light in someone's life?

DAY 18 • ACTIVITY #3:
RANDOM ACT OF KINDNESS

Look around you and notice where a kind act could make a difference. Here are some ideas!

1. Bring cookies to a friend.

2. Write an encouraging note to a family member.

3. Offer to walk the neighbor's dog or get their mail while they're out of town.

4. Wash the dishes or do another chore without being asked.

5. Help your little brother or sister with their homework or a household chore.

6. Clean up trash at a local park or playground.

7. Write a note to a favorite teacher telling him/her how they encourage you.

8. Clean out your closet and make a pile of clothes and/or toys to donate.

9. Return someone's cart at the grocery store.

10. Buy extra school supplies and bring them to your teacher to use in the classroom.

If anyone, then, knows the good they ought
to do and doesn't do it, it is sin for them.

JAMES 4:17

Have you ever seen someone stand by when a terrible thing
was happening? Someone who did nothing as another
person was bullied or hurt or mistreated?

There are so many opportunities where we can step up and
encourage those around us to treat others with kindness.
Edmund Burke, a philosopher and politician from the 1700s,
once said, "All that is necessary for the triumph of evil is that
good men do nothing." When we are silent, we may feel like
we are innocent because we aren't the ones being mean, but
often, doing nothing is the same as doing something wrong.
There are times when we need to be the ones to step up in a
situation and do or say the right thing.

We should never pass up an opportunity to act with kindness,
mercy, and compassion. We should always look for ways to
spread joy and kindness to the world around us. God will
give you the courage you need to be a bright light of hope to
those around you. A little bit of kindness can go a long way in
changing someone's life. Don't ever underestimate how God
might use your willingness to step up and speak out.

TAKEAWAY

We need to speak up and do good in our family, our schools, and with our friends. We need to treat others with kindness, gentleness, and respect and encourage others to do the same.

WRITE ABOUT IT ...

Was there a time that you stood up for someone who was being treated unfairly? What are some other ways you can help those in need?

"If I speak in the tongues of men and of angels,
but have not love, I am only a resounding gong or
a clanging cymbal. If I have the gift of prophecy
and can fathom all mysteries and all knowledge,
and if I have a faith that can move mountains,
but have not love, I am nothing. If I give all I
possess to the poor and surrender my body to
the flames, but have not love, I gain nothing."

1 CORINTHIANS 13:1–3

Chances are that you would never go to a musical concert where the conductor has the percussion section bang cymbals over and over again without accompanying other instruments. It would just be loud noise without any melody or beauty to soften the sound. We all have people in our lives who may be hard for us to love, but God tells us that without love we are just like those clanging cymbals. We are just creating noise, but no real beauty. We have people all around us who may not ever know the love that God offers unless they see it through us first. We live in a world that is desperate for something or someone that looks and sounds different from all the other noise, and the best way for us to do that is to love those around us.

When we begin to understand how much God loves us, we become secure in knowing that God has good things for us. This security in his love will be the key to helping love the people around us in a way that makes a difference. We need to love the people that God puts in our path.

We will make the difference by loving others, and showing them a glimpse of how much they are loved by God through our actions towards them. Let's work hard to make love the loudest voice and action in our life.

TAKEAWAY

Without love, we have nothing. We need to love the people that God has put in our lives.

WRITE ABOUT IT ...

What are some ways you can show love to someone in your family or in your class at school?

_____

_____

_____

_____

DAY 21

"For I know the plans I have for you," declares
the Lord, "plans to prosper you and not to harm
you, plans to give you hope and a future. Then
you will call on me and come and pray to me,
and I will listen to you. You will seek me and find
me when you seek me with all your heart."

JEREMIAH 29:11–13

Your relationship with Jesus is as uniquely yours as your
personality. We can spend a lot of time thinking we
should be more like this person or that person or hear from
God in a certain way, but he made us all unique. He's made
you to be you. If God was only after one type of relationship
with one type of person, it probably would have been a whole
lot easier for him to create just one person and be done with it.

But God made each of us to do different things based on the
gifts and talents he has given us. Not one of our lives will look
the same as someone else's because he has a future and a hope
planned specifically for YOU. Sometimes it's hard to know
what that looks like or what he has in store for us, but if we
read our Bible and ask him to show us what he would have
us do, then we won't miss all the good things he has in store
for our lives. We need to seek him with all our hearts through
prayer and reading his words so that we will know his voice
and learn the way that we should go.

TAKEAWAY

God has a future planned that is just for you and it will be more than you could ever do on your own.

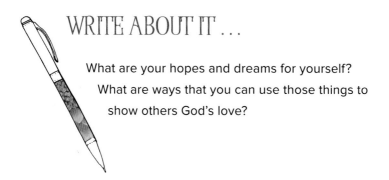

WRITE ABOUT IT . . .

What are your hopes and dreams for yourself? What are ways that you can use those things to show others God's love?

_____

_____

_____

_____

_____

_____

DAY 22

I will lead the blind by ways they have not
known, along unfamiliar paths I will guide them;
I will turn the darkness into light before them
and make the rough places smooth. These are
the things I will do; I will not forsake them.

ISAIAH 42:16

Have you ever played a game like pin the tail on the donkey where you've been blindfolded and had to find your way? Or have you ever been camping and had to find your way in the dark over rough ground? It's hard to know where we are supposed to go or see the right path when everything is dark around us.

There are times when life will feel this way. Maybe you have some friendships that are changing, a teacher that you don't really like, or things in your house are just really difficult and you feel like your parents don't understand you.

God knows we will have times that our path will feel dark and unfamiliar and he wants you to know that you will never walk that road alone. When we trust God in these hard, rough places in life, he will make them feel smooth. And when it all seems dark in your world, his love for you will light the way. God will never leave you.

 TAKEAWAY

At times, life can be hard and we feel surrounded by darkness. But God is always with us and will always put light in our path when we seek him.

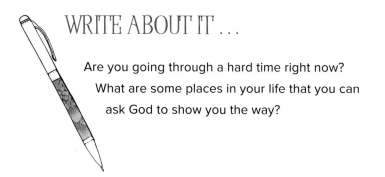 WRITE ABOUT IT . . .

Are you going through a hard time right now? What are some places in your life that you can ask God to show you the way?

DAY 23

When you have eaten and are satisfied, praise
the LORD your God for the good land he has given
you. Be careful that you do not forget the LORD
your God, failing to observe his commands, his
laws and his decrees that I am giving you this day.

DEUTERONOMY 8:10–11

God knows us so well and he knows that we often have a
tendency to quit spending time with him when everything in our lives is going well. That's why one of his warnings
to the children of Israel was that they not forget to praise him
after they reached the Promised Land.

When you pray, do you spend any time thanking him for all
he has done for you? You would probably never call or text a
friend every day and give them a list of things you want without saying thank you. When someone does something nice for
you, you are probably quick to tell them thank you!

You need to remember to be equally faithful to telling God
thank you. When you take the time to remember all the ways
he has been good to you, it helps you to be content and find
the joy in your life. You become more aware than ever of the
blessings God has given you.

TAKEAWAY

Remember to take time to thank God for all he has done in your life and to give him praise for your blessings.

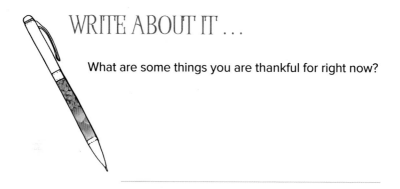

WRITE ABOUT IT . . .

What are some things you are thankful for right now?

DAY 24 • ACTIVITY #4:
A GLOW LIGHT

Make a glow light out of a mason jar as a reminder to let your light shine bright.

- Jar (any clean jar will do)
- Glow-in-the-dark paint (use several colors if you can)
- Paintbrushes
- Scrap paper
- White school glue (optional)
- Glitter (optional)

Set up your supplies. Place a piece of scrap paper down and squirt some of your paints onto the paper.

Start painting your jar with the glow-in-the-dark paint. Use several colors of paint. Paint your jar starting at the bottom of the inside, dabbing small dots using your brush. If you have several brushes, simply alternate your brushes and paint colors to get a random multi-color effect. Once you have finished painting the inside of your jar, it needs to dry.

To activate the glow-in-the-dark paint, you need to allow your jar to soak up UV rays, so it is best to plan this project when you have time to let it sit in the sun for at least an hour.

This is optional, but you can cover the jar lid with a thin layer of glue and sprinkle it with glitter for a glittery effect. Do this step over a piece of scrap paper that you can throw away. Shake off the excess glitter and allow the lid to dry.

Wait until it's dark or go into a dark closet and watch how your creation lights up!

DAY 25

The Lord had said to Abram, "Go from your
country, your people and your father's
household to the land I will show you" . . . So
Abram went, as the Lord had told him; and
Lot went with him. Abram was seventy-five
years old when he set out from Harran.

GENESIS 12:1, 4

Abram had no idea what God had in store for him when
he asked him to leave his country and head toward the
land of Canaan. But Abram packed up his camels, loaded the
family up, and made his way toward a strange land.

What made him do it? His faith that God wasn't going to do
him wrong or lead him to a place with no provisions for him
and his family. His faith in God's promises.

What if Abram had stayed? We don't know the answer to
that, other than God wouldn't have been able to use Abram
the way he did. God has plans for all of us, plans that he has
known before we ever took a breath, but he never forces us to
do anything. We take our own steps, whether they are toward
his will or away from it.

But usually those steps require faith. Our job is to take steps
of faith, away from what we know, toward what God is building with our lives. He never promises it will be easy, but he
promises that with him all things are possible.

 TAKEAWAY

Often God calls us to take steps of faith that may seem scary because they are new and different. But he will always bring us something better than anything we leave behind.

 WRITE ABOUT IT . . .

Has there ever been a time you felt like you were supposed to let go of something so that God could do something new in your life?

DAY 26

As soon as he had finished speaking to Saul,
the soul of Jonathan was knit to the soul of
David, and Jonathan loved him as his own soul.

1 SAMUEL 18:1 (ESV)

One of the best stories of friendship in the Bible is the story of Jonathan and David. David was a young shepherd boy whom God had chosen as the next king of Israel and Jonathan was the current king's son. In a way, this situation makes them the unlikeliest of friends. But the Bible states that their souls were knit together, which means their hearts and lives were bound to each other. That's a powerful bond. God brought them into each other's lives because God knew how much they would need each other in the years to come. God brought them together to make them stronger.

That's often how real friendship is formed. God brings people into our lives and we recognize some version of ourselves in someone else. Maybe we laugh at the same quirky things, love the same music, or have other friends in common. Or maybe you just end up sitting next to each other in math class and before you know it, you realize how much you look forward to seeing each other every day. No matter how friendship starts, it is a valuable and necessary thing in our lives—to open up to another person that you can completely trust with your heart and begin to make each other stronger people than you were before.

Jonathan and David had that kind of friendship. They built each other up and treated each other with loyalty, kindness, and generosity. That's real friendship. That's what it means to have your soul knit to another person.

 TAKEAWAY

God brings friends into our lives who will build us up and that we can love and encourage.

 WRITE ABOUT IT . . .

Who are your closest friends right now? How do they encourage you or make you be a better person?

_____

_____

_____

_____

> Ask and it will be given to you; seek and you
> will find; knock and the door will be opened
> to you. For everyone who asks receives;
> the one who seeks finds; and to the one
> who knocks, the door will be opened.
>
> MATTHEW 7:7–8

Have you ever really wanted something or prayed something would happen a certain way and then it didn't work out the way you hoped? One of the hardest things to understand is when God doesn't answer our prayers the way we want or believe he should.

Sometimes our disappointment in the way God chose to answer a past prayer may keep us from asking him for other things. But we are specifically told to ask and seek God for things in our lives. We don't learn who God is by just accepting everything that comes our way, but by opening our hearts to hearing his voice and knowing he always has our best interests in mind. God wants to hear from you. He wants to hear your hopes and dreams. And every time you take the time to talk to him, you are giving yourself the chance to get to know him better.

When you stop to consider that God is beyond wise and loves you more than you can imagine, the fact that he tells you to ask him for what you need is an invitation that you would be silly to turn down. Trust God and ask him for the things you want in your life, and trust his goodness even when the outcome is different than what you expected.

TAKEAWAY

God invites us to ask him for the things we want, need, or hope to see happen in our lives.

WRITE ABOUT IT . . .

What are some things you are praying for right now? How have you seen God answer those prayers? What about a time God answered something differently than you hoped? Can you can see now that it was for the best?

DAY 28

But David said to Saul, "Your servant has been keeping his father's sheep. When a lion or a bear came and carried off a sheep from the flock, I went after it, struck it and rescued the sheep from its mouth. When it turned on me, I seized it by its hair, struck it and killed it. Your servant has killed both the lion and the bear; this uncircumcised Philistine will be like one of them, because he has defied the armies of the living God. The LORD who rescued me from the paw of the lion and the paw of the bear will rescue me from the hand of this Philistine."

1 SAMUEL 17:34–37

Before David was ever a king, he was a shepherd. His job was to watch over a flock of sheep and to keep them safe from anything that might try to harm them. Eventually, God had bigger things for David and he found himself facing a huge giant named Goliath who even the bravest men in the Israelite army were afraid to face. Yet David ran toward Goliath with confidence that God would give him the strength to win the battle.

It was in the pasture, herding and taking care of sheep, that David learned how to be king. He learned responsibility, how to be a provider and a protector, and how to throw a stone. Most importantly, he sat in the quiet places with God and learned how much God would always take care of him.

It's sometimes in the quiet, small places that you learn to hear God's voice and trust him. Those are often the times in life when he's preparing you for the bigger challenges ahead so that you can remember that he has always taken care of you in the past.

TAKEAWAY

God uses things you are doing right now to prepare your heart and mind for the future. He will always be faithful to help us face our challenges.

WRITE ABOUT IT . . .

What is a challenge that you are going through right now? Can you think back to a time in the past when God taught you something that can help you get through whatever you are facing now?

DAY 29

You intended to harm me, but God intended
it for good to accomplish what is now
being done, the saving of many lives.

GENESIS 50:20

In the story of Joseph, we quickly learn that he was his father's favorite. His father made him a coat of many colors to show his love for his son, and his brothers grew jealous of him. Then Joseph had dreams of his brothers bowing down to him, which made them hate him even more. So they threw him into a pit and sold him into slavery. But God was always with him and even though it took twenty years, Joseph rose to the second highest position in all of Egypt and ended up saving the very brothers who had betrayed him.

That probably wasn't the life Joseph had planned. Your life won't always go the way you plan. Sometimes faithfulness to God and his word sets us on a course where our situation gets worse, not better. And those are the times when knowing God and his promise to be good and faithful is more important than ever. Faith in God is what gets us through the hard times when things don't turn out the way we hoped or planned.

But what we learn at the end of Joseph's story is that God used every bit of it for a good purpose. If not for all the things that Joseph went through, he never would have ended up saving the people of Israel. God does the same thing in our lives.

He uses all that we have been through to prepare us for the things he has for us in the future. Often what doesn't make sense in the moment is the very thing that helps us become what God is making us to be.

TAKEAWAY

God uses the hard things in our life to help us become who he created us to be.

WRITE ABOUT IT...

Think about a time when you went through something difficult. Can you see now that God used it in a good way in your life?

_____

_____

_____

_____

DAY 30 • ACTIVITY #5:
MAKE A WORSHIP SONG PLAYLIST

>>>>>>>> ∞∞— • —∞∞ •••

When we are going through hard times or life just doesn't make sense, it can help to fill your mind with God's word and remind yourself of God's love and faithfulness. Listening to worship songs is a great way to do this and you can share your list with friends.

Here are ten suggestions of songs you could find to put on your list:

1. A song about the greatness of God

2. A song written and sung by a teenage artist

3. A song about God's faithfulness

4. A song about how much God loves you

5. A song about how God answers prayer

6. A song about God's grace

7. An instrumental song where you can just focus on what God is saying to you

8. A song about the holiness of God

9. A song that best describes how you feel about God in your life

10. A song that you could use to encourage others

> When the angel of the Lord appeared to Gideon,
> he said, "The Lord is with you, mighty warrior."
>
> JUDGES 6:12

In the book of Judges, Israel has been invaded by the Midianites and there is a man named Gideon who is threshing wheat in a winepress. Normally, he'd thresh his wheat out in the open, but Gideon is afraid of the Midianites and so he is hiding in this winepress.

While he is hiding out, an angel appears to him and says, "The Lord is with you, mighty warrior." Mighty warrior? Gideon is hiding. He's threshing his wheat in fear and yet the angel calls him a mighty warrior.

The angel has come to tell him that God is going to use him to deliver the Israelites from Midian. At first, Gideon doesn't believe it. In the end, Gideon ends up being exactly what the angel called him—a mighty warrior. He defeats the Midianites using only three hundred men. Do you see what God did there? He called Gideon to something he could have never imagined for himself. That's what God does, he can turn someone who is afraid into a mighty warrior who will stand up for what is right.

God sees what you can't see. He sees gifts and talents in you when you feel like there's nothing. You see all your fears and weaknesses, but he looks at you and sees something he can use for his plans and purposes. He looks at you and sees a mighty warrior.

TAKEAWAY

God sees so much more in you than you see in yourself.

WRITE ABOUT IT...

What are some ways God could use you to make a difference in the lives of the people around you? What keeps you from letting him use you to do those things?

DAY 32

You are the light of the world. A town
built on a hill cannot be hidden.

MATTHEW 5:14

When Jesus said these words to his disciples, he was comparing their lives to a city built on a hill. In those days, a city lit up on a hill would have been a welcome sight for weary travelers, a sign that they were nearing a place where they could find a warm bed and a good meal.

We live in a world where bullying has gone on from the beginning of time and has never been easier now that people can hide behind a keyboard and say things to you that they'd never say to your face. Jesus's words are a reminder that you need to be a city on a hill who treats others with kindness and respect even when they are different from you and you don't agree with them. You live in a world where darkness is everywhere and people are desperately looking for safety and light.

When you realize that God has put you in this time and in this generation for a very specific and unique reason, you realize that instead of finding power or making yourself feel better by making someone else feel small and insignificant, you were created to be light.

This is what it means to be a city on a hill. You are called to be a place of hope, safety, and comfort where those around you can come and find rest, love, and light in the middle of a dark world.

TAKEAWAY

You are called to be a safe place for others to find rest and hope in this world.

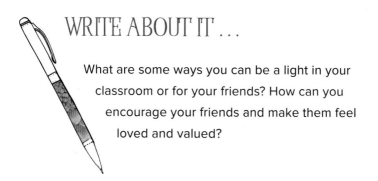

WRITE ABOUT IT . . .

What are some ways you can be a light in your classroom or for your friends? How can you encourage your friends and make them feel loved and valued?

DAY 33

His master replied, 'Well done, good and faithful
servant! You have been faithful with a few
things; I will put you in charge of many things.
Come and share your master's happiness!'

MATTHEW 25:21

In the parable about the master and the bags of gold, we see
three different scenarios. The master gives one man five bags
of gold and the man returns to share that he has gained five
more. The next man is given two bags of gold and comes back
with an additional two bags of gold. And the last man says that
he was afraid so he just buried the gold.

There are things you are given in life like talent, time, money,
skills, and other resources. God has gifted you but it is up to
you to decide how you will use those gifts. Will you take a
chance and jump into what he has called you to do, to be, and
to stand for? Or will you let fear get the best of you and bury
what you've been given?

God is like the master. He is waiting to see if you will be
faithful to use what you've been given to bring glory to God.

Don't underestimate the impact you can have in the lives of
those around you when you use your gifts. God very pur-
posely created you for this time and in this generation, so do
your best to not bury what you've been given.

 TAKEAWAY

God has given you many gifts and talents. It's up to you if you will use them wisely or hide them away.

WRITE ABOUT IT . . .

What are some ways you can let your gifts shine
and use what God has given you to make a
difference? Have you ever hidden something
away and then realized that it was a mistake?

_____

_____

_____

_____

_____

_____

But he knows the way that I take; when he has tested me, I will come forth as gold. My feet have closely followed his steps; I have kept to his way without turning aside.

JOB 23:10–11

Several years ago, Texas was in the middle of the worst drought in its history and there was huge wildfire that spread through a little town called Bastrop. Just a year later, you could see signs that there had been a fire, but there was also new green growth all along the roadside.

That's often how God works in your life. Sometimes you let all this stuff in without even realizing it. You may have some unhealthy friendships or habits you've developed. And sometimes you have to burn away some of the old and dead things in your life to feel healthy again. New, healthy growth often shows up best after your heart has been through a time when you've had to let some things go that weren't good for you. The most beautiful things come after the fire, when God can do new things in your life because the old junk is no longer in the way.

And just like gold, God uses the fires in your life to shape you and bring out everything you need to shine and see the beauty that only he can bring.

TAKEAWAY

There are sometimes old habits or things in your life that are keeping you from growing into all God wants you to become.

WRITE ABOUT IT . . .

Are there any old habits or patterns you have in your life that are keeping you from letting God move in your life? How can you take steps to let go of some of those things?

When they arrived, Samuel saw Eliab and thought,
"Surely the Lord's anointed stands here before
the Lord." But the Lord said to Samuel, "Do not
consider his appearance or his height, for I have
rejected him. The Lord does not look at the
things people look at. People look at the outward
appearance, but the Lord looks at the heart."

1 SAMUEL 16:6–7

When Samuel went to find the next king, he asked Jesse if these were all his sons and Jesse replied that his youngest son, David, wasn't there because he was tending sheep. They called for David. When Samuel saw him, he knew that David was God's chosen king so he anointed him right then and there.

The thing is that Jesse was so sure that Samuel wouldn't be interested in David that he didn't even call him in from the pasture. But God saw David's heart and knew he was up for the task even when David's own family didn't.

Have you ever felt that way? Overlooked? Forgotten? Like you've been left out in the pasture because no one thought you were worthy of being called in?

The anointing of David is a reminder to not let others determine what God wants to do through you. Don't let other people, even family members, make you feel like you aren't worthy. God is absolutely calling you to something. He has a plan and a purpose for you.

TAKEAWAY

God sees you even when you feel like you've been overlooked by the rest of the world.

WRITE ABOUT IT . . .

Do you feel like God has a purpose and a plan for you? What are some ways you feel like he has made you special?

DAY 36 • ACTIVITY #6:
TIME CAPSULE

A time capsule can be a great way to remember the past. You will be able to look back at your time capsule in ten years and see all the ways God has answered your prayers and is making you into the person he created you to be.

1. Find a container. An old coffee can or a shoe box will do. You can decorate it if you'd like.

2. Fill it with things or memories that are important to you, maybe a favorite picture or small toy.

3. Write a letter to your future self about who you are now and what is important to you. What job would you like to have when you are older?

4. Make a list of some of your favorite things: your favorite teacher, your favorite subject in school, your best friends, your favorite songs.

5. Ask your mom or dad to write a letter to you that you can put in the time capsule.

6. Write a description of what your life is like right now. What does your normal day look like? What are the activities you enjoy? What are some things you are praying for?

7. Describe trends or clothing that are popular right now.

8. Print out some news articles or cut out articles from magazines about things that are going on in the world right now.

9. Make a list of ten words that best describe you and your hopes and dreams for yourself.

10. Put the time capsule in a safe place. Maybe store it in a box in the attic or in the top of your closet to make sure you don't lose it.

DAY 37

Blessed is the one who does not walk in step
with the wicked or stand in the way that sinners
take or sit in the company of mockers, but
whose delight is in the law of the Lord, and
who meditates on his law day and night. That
person is like a tree planted by streams of water,
which yields its fruit in season and whose leaf
does not wither—whatever they do prospers.

PSALMS 1:1–3

Psalm 1:3 says that a person who spends time in God's
Word is like a tree planted by streams of water. A tree
that is planted near the water has everything it needs to grow
strong and to bear fruit. In your life that kind of fruit looks
like facing your fears, being kind to others, not being selfish,
and finding joy in life.

Have you ever watched a big tree in the middle of a storm? It may
bend and a few limbs may even fall, but the roots of the tree stand
firm. A good, healthy tree has roots that go down deep into the
ground and sustain it even during the toughest times.

When you spend time reading God's Word and taking the
time to bring your worries and fears to him, he gives you the
kind of strength that comes from knowing that even when
you face scary or hard times, you are like a tree that has been
given all the nutrients and strength it needs to get through

any storms it may face and that leads to knowing that you are exactly where God wants you to be and doing what he is calling you to do.

TAKEAWAY

When you spend time in God's Word, you become stronger and live a life that is richer and better because you are walking the right path.

WRITE ABOUT IT . . .

What are some areas where you see fruit in your life when you spend time with God? How does it help you make better choices or be a better friend to those around you?

Then Saul dressed David in his own tunic. He put
a coat of armor on him and a bronze helmet on
his head. David fastened on his sword over the
tunic and tried walking around, because he was
not used to them. "I cannot go in these," he said
to Saul, "because I am not used to them." So he
took them off. Then he took his staff in his hand,
chose five smooth stones from the stream, put
them in the pouch of his shepherd's bag and, with
his sling in his hand, approached the Philistine.

1 SAMUEL 17: 38–40

You've probably heard the story about David killing Goliath
at least a few times. It's a literary classic, probably because
it's everything we love in a story. A small shepherd boy who
was just delivering lunch, an ugly giant who was tormenting
an army, a little bit of trash talk, and then triumph over evil.

Saul tries to equip David for his battle with Goliath by giving
him his own armor. And this isn't just any armor. Saul is the
king so you know it was all made of the finest materials man can
make. Yet David quickly realized that it wasn't going to work
for him. So David grabbed his staff and five smooth stones as he
approached Goliath. And, well, you know the rest of the story.

It's a reminder that sometimes when we face big challenges in
life, we are waiting for God to give us big, fancy ways to fight

them. Surely big problems call for elaborate solutions, right? Except that they don't. Sometimes it's as simple as remembering that the God of the armies of Israel fights for you and so it's never about your ability to fight a giant. All you need is to remember that you never go into battle alone.

TAKEAWAY

When we face battles, God has already given you everything you need because he goes ahead of us to fight for us.

WRITE ABOUT IT . . .

What are some battles you are facing right now?
How is God helping you get through them?

DAY 39

For you were once darkness, but now you
are light in the Lord. Live as children of
light (for the fruit of the light consists in all
goodness, righteousness and truth).

EPHESIANS 5:8–9

A couple of years ago, the Clemson University football team won the National Championship and their coach, Dabo Swinney, told reporters after the game that he just kept encouraging his players to "let the light inside of them shine brighter than the light that was on them." It's a great reminder that it's the light of Christ inside of you that makes a difference in the world and never a spotlight on yourself.

When you let the light of Christ shine on you it helps you focus on others and pay less attention to yourself. You begin to think about things like, where can I help? How can I encourage someone? Who can I reach out to with a kind word? Because you remember what it feels like to walk in darkness and fear and loneliness. You know that feeling of hearing a voice tell you you're not good enough or valuable or that your life doesn't mean much.

But that's where Jesus comes in. He is the light in your life. He shines his light in us and on us and it's up to you to be the light in your little corner of the world.

TAKEAWAY

Let the light of Jesus shine bright in your life so that you can impact the people around you and make a difference in your family and with your friends.

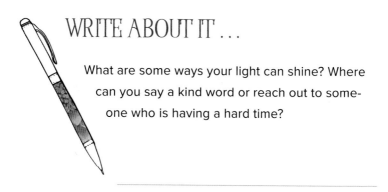

WRITE ABOUT IT . . .

What are some ways your light can shine? Where can you say a kind word or reach out to someone who is having a hard time?

I am the vine; you are the branches. If you
remain in me and I in you, you will bear much
fruit; apart from me you can do nothing.

JOHN 15: 5

Have you ever seen an orange tree go through the process of growing oranges? It starts with little blossoms that show up all over the tree and then the blossoms eventually give way to the beginnings of the fruit. The oranges start out as tiny green balls that continue to grow bigger and bigger until they resemble limes. Then their color begins to change from a deep green to a light yellow and then, finally, orange.

But here's what is interesting about watching a tree go through all the cycles of producing fruit; it isn't stressed about the process. Its roots go deep, the branches are connected to the trunk, and that's all it needs to blossom and grow.

It's easy to get stressed out about your life and whether or not you are producing fruit. Are you making good decisions? Are you patient enough? Do you need to be a better friend? You are a lot like an orange tree. When you are connected to the source of all that you need, you can't help but bear fruit. And, sometimes, just like a little tree, it's hard to see the fruit and the fullness of what you will become until, suddenly, it becomes clear that this was what you were intended to be from the very beginning. It just took remaining rooted to the tree to get there.

TAKEAWAY

When you remain in Christ, your life will show the fruits of the spirit like love, gentleness, self-control, and patience.

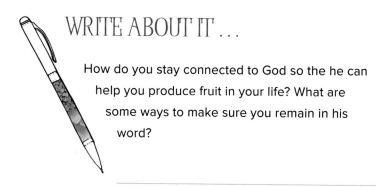

WRITE ABOUT IT . . .

How do you stay connected to God so the he can help you produce fruit in your life? What are some ways to make sure you remain in his word?

DAY 41

Jesus replied, "Anyone who drinks this water
will soon become thirsty again. But those
who drink the water I give will never be
thirsty again. It becomes a fresh, bubbling
spring within them, giving them eternal life."
"Please, sir," the woman said, "give me this
water! Then I'll never be thirsty again, and
I won't have to come here to get water."

JOHN 4:13–15 (NLT)

Jesus had been traveling all morning when he came to a well around noon. It was hot and dusty, he needed a drink, and that's when he came upon a woman. Here's what Jesus knew; she was at the well at the wrong time of the day. Women typically gathered water in the morning. But she chose that time because she thought no one else would be there. Except that on this day, Jesus is there.

You may think life has brought you to a certain point because you're just looking for water, but Jesus meets you there because he knows you are looking for security and love just like the woman at the well. Jesus shows up in your life, wherever your well may be, and offers you living water, which is his love for you. He offers you everything you need, even though sometimes you keep looking for all these other things to fill you up. He looks at you with love and asks, "Aren't you ready for the real thing that will make you feel full?"

What are the wells in your life where you are looking for something that you think will make you feel full? Jesus meets us at the wells of our lives and gives us everything we've been looking for and so much more. Trust him.

TAKEAWAY

Jesus meets you exactly where you need him and he offers you his love. His love is the only thing that will fill you up and make you feel complete.

WRITE ABOUT IT . . .

What are some things you try to use in your life to feel full or like you matter? Where can you trust Jesus to really fill you up with love and security that lasts?

MAKE A BIRDFEEDER

This is a great way to not only enjoy God's creation, but to remind yourself that God cares for even the smallest creatures. Look at all the different colors and patterns that God gives different species of birds and think about how he uniquely created you and cares for all the little details of your life.

MATERIALS

- Orange
- 4 pieces of yarn or string, cut into 24" long pieces
- Birdseed

1. With a sharp knife, cut the orange in half and scoop out the insides.

2. Poke 4 small holes on opposite sides, about $1/2$" from the top edge of each half of the orange.

3. Thread one piece of yarn or string through a hole, and out the opposite end. Repeat with the second piece of yarn in the remaining holes. (It will make an "X".)

4. Gather the ends together and tie in a knot. Repeat with the other half.

5. Fill with birdseed and hang from a sturdy tree branch outside.

"In the future, when your children ask you,
'What do these stones mean?' tell them that
the flow of the Jordan was cut off before
the ark of the covenant of the LORD. When
it crossed the Jordan, the waters of the
Jordan were cut off. These stones are to be
a memorial to the people of Israel forever."

JOSHUA 4:6–7

In Joshua 3 the Israelites are preparing to cross the Jordan River. As the priests stepped into the edge of the river, carrying the Ark of the Covenant, the water stopped flowing and the priests stood on dry ground in the middle of the Jordan, until the entire nation of Israel had crossed safely. When they reached the other side, Joshua explained that God had told him they needed to put up stones to remember what God had done for them as a sign of God's faithfulness.

It's important to have your own personal remembrance stones. Stories of the times in your life when God proved himself faithful. Sometimes when you look at the little pieces of your life, they don't appear to be much until you look back at the big picture and see all the ways that God helped you through a hard time. This helps you remember he is always true to his word and makes all things beautiful in his time. There is always an answer when we call on him.

These are the stories you can tell when people ask you why you believe in God, why you trust in a God you cannot see.

TAKEAWAY

It's good to have reminders in your life about the times that God took care of you or provided a solution to a problem you were facing.

WRITE ABOUT IT...

Take a few minutes to write down your own re-membrance stones to help you remember when God has been faithful to take care of you.

DAY 44

Can any one of you by worrying
add a single hour to your life?

MATTHEW 6:27

We all have times in our life when we worry. The problem is that worrying usually means spending a lot of time feeling anxious about something that may never happen.

It gives you a feeling of control when you can plan out everything in your life, but that's not really how life works. It's so easy to worry about your grades, your friends, or what you are going to do in the future. But many of the things you worry about never actually happen.

And, even if they do, they are almost never as bad as you imagined them to be. You can never account for how God will take care of you if you actually find yourself in the middle of the worst thing you could have imagined.

Life can be hard and scary and difficult, but worrying isn't going to help. When you keep your eyes on Jesus, he can help you keep your worrying in check. Know that God has you in the palm of his hand. Trusting him is the only thing that will give you real peace.

TAKEAWAY

Worrying about things instead of trusting God with all the pieces of your life isn't the best way to go through life.

WRITE ABOUT IT . . .

What are some things you are worried about right now? Make a list of your worries and then ask God to help you trust him and have peace about each situation and the outcome.

DAY 45

A heart at peace gives life to the
body, but envy rots the bones.

PROVERBS 14:30

Our human nature causes us to spend a lot of time looking around at what everyone else has or does. Social media has made this worse because you have constant access to how great everyone else's life looks compared to your own. It's so easy for envy and jealousy to creep in, causing you to lose any peace you have in your life as you focus on what you don't have instead of what you have been given.

When you begin to feel those feelings of jealousy pop up, it's good to take time to think of all the things you have in your life that make you feel thankful. Think about your friends, your family, your teachers, or talents you have been given. Our lives aren't supposed to look like anyone else's. We were created to be unique.

When your focus shifts from envying others to seeing what God has for you and the unique gifts he has placed in your life, you can experience real peace, real contentment, and real joy that isn't based on external things.

 TAKEAWAY

Jealousy never serves a good purpose in your life and can make you forget about the good things God has given you.

WRITE ABOUT IT . . .

When was the last time you felt jealous of someone? What was it about their life that made you feel that way? What are some ways you can ask God to help you focus on what you have instead of what you don't have?

When the Philistines banded together at a
place where there was a field full of lentils,
Israel's troops fled from them. But Shammah
took his stand in the middle of the field. He
defended it and struck the Philistines down,
and the LORD brought about a great victory.

2 SAMUEL 23:11–12

When the Philistines attacked, the Israelite army ran away,
but Shammah chose to take a stand right there in that
field and defend it. Shammah didn't compromise, he didn't
back down. He knew it was a battle worth fighting.

There comes a time in your life when you have to make the
decision to stand up and fight instead of backing down.
You have ground in your life that you will have to choose to
protect. God has a purpose for every part of your life so the
greatest trick the enemy can play on you is to convince you
that something isn't worth the fight.

And here's the encouraging part. Shammah took his stand in
that field of lentils but the scripture says that it was the Lord
who brought about the victory. Shammah's faith was never in
his own ability to fight, but his faith that God was with him
and would fight for him. The next time you find yourself facing
a fight and you know you are supposed to stand your ground,
remember that God goes before you and will fight for you.

TAKEAWAY

There will be times when God will call you to take a stand in your life and fight for what you believe in.

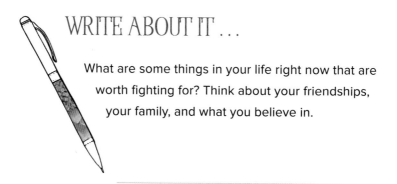

WRITE ABOUT IT...

What are some things in your life right now that are worth fighting for? Think about your friendships, your family, and what you believe in.

DAY 47

Consider it pure joy, my brothers and sisters,
whenever you face trials of many kinds,
because you know that the testing of your faith
produces perseverance. Let perseverance
finish its work so that you may be mature
and complete, not lacking anything.

JAMES 1:2–4

Many years ago, before we knew about the importance of things like protecting the environment, people used to throw their trash into the ocean.

We know better now than to throw our trash in the ocean, but all those glass bottles that were tossed in the ocean over the years ended up being broken into shards of glass as they were pounded by the waves. They get tossed about and hit sand and rocks and these sharp, jagged pieces of glass eventually get polished into smooth, polished pieces that look like jewels and become little treasures that wash up on the beaches.

These pieces are called sea glass. Your life is often like these broken pieces. You may have sharp edges and feel broken, like there are parts of your life that make you feel as though you have no purpose. But God uses the waves and rocks in your life, the hard times that often seem like they are going to be the final straw that will break you, to create something new and even more beautiful than what you once were.

He hones out your sharp edges, polishes your heart, and makes you into his very own beautiful work of art. Because it's often after you've gone through the hardest situations and problems that you are the best version of yourself.

 TAKEAWAY

God uses the hard times in your life to polish you and make you into someone better, stronger, and more beautiful than you were before.

WRITE ABOUT IT . . .

What are some ways God has used hard times in your life to build your character or make you stronger?

DAY 48 • ACTIVITY #8:
AN OUTDOOR SCAVENGER HUNT

1. Decide when and where you want to have your scavenger hunt.

2. Send out emails or text an invite to your friends. Invite enough people to have at least two small groups.

3. Give each team a list of items that they need to find. Here are some suggestions:
   - a bird feather
   - an acorn
   - a pinecone
   - a rock
   - something yellow
   - something that floats
   - a flower
   - a penny or another coin
   - a piece of trash
   - two leaves that look the same

4. Set a time limit (maybe an hour) for each team to find as many items as they can and return to their starting location.

5. Have fun and use the time to get to know each other better!

Be kind and compassionate to one
another, forgiving each other, just
as in Christ, God forgave you.

EPHESIANS 4:32

If you've ever been hurt by someone then you know that one of the hardest things to do is forgive that person and move on from the way they treated you. It's so easy to hold on to your anger and bitterness over the situation because, honestly, sometimes it just feels good to be angry for a while. But God calls you to be different and to handle these situations in a way that doesn't always seem to make sense.

When someone says something that is unkind or untrue about you or behind your back, your gut reaction is usually to respond with something equally unkind. But God wants you to be kind and forgive them no matter how they have treated you. This doesn't mean that they weren't wrong, but God knows that when you choose to forgive it allows you to move on from that situation with a clean heart.

You can't change how other people choose to act, but you can choose how you respond to it. When you remember all the times God has forgiven you for being wrong, it becomes easier to extend that same kindness and grace to the people around you. And when you respond in love, kindness, and forgiveness, you are letting others see a glimpse of what Jesus' love looks like.

TAKEAWAY

Treat others with kindness and compassion and forgive them when they hurt you.

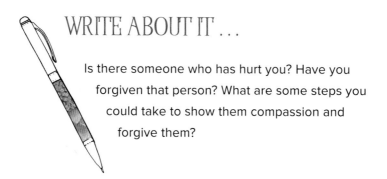

WRITE ABOUT IT...

Is there someone who has hurt you? Have you forgiven that person? What are some steps you could take to show them compassion and forgive them?

DAY 50

But the fruit of the Spirit is love, joy,
peace, forbearance, kindness, goodness,
faithfulness, gentleness and self-control.

GALATIANS 5:22–23

When you think of fruit, the first thing that probably comes to mind is a banana, an orange, or an apple. Or maybe you like more exotic fruit like a pomegranate or kiwi. But when you are filled with the Spirit of God, you have another kind of fruit in your life, things like kindness, joy, patience, and self-control, that you are called to show others.

This isn't always easy. In fact, sometimes it can be really hard to have patience and self-control. Many times, when you feel angry or hurt, the last thing you want to do is find a way to let God help you feel joy or self-control. And here's the thing, God knows that about you. He knows that you can't do it on your own.

When you let his words and his light shine in your heart, his spirit helps you produce good fruit. It's the same way that a healthy tree is always going to grow fruit that tastes much better than a tree that is sick or dying. Best of all, you can always run to God when you are having a hard time seeing any fruit in your life or are struggling to be gentle or kind. He will give you the strength you need to produce the kind of spiritual fruit that can make all the difference to your friends, family, and anyone else in your life.

TAKEAWAY

You are called to bear fruit in your life which means you treat others with kindness, peace, and patience.

WRITE ABOUT IT...

What fruit do you feel comes easily for you? Where do you struggle to bear good fruit? Ask God to help you with any place in your life where you are having a hard time showing his love.

> Do nothing out of selfish ambition or vain conceit. Rather, in humility value others above yourselves, not looking to your own interests but each of you to the interests of the others.
>
> PHILIPPIANS 2:3–4

It is so easy to be selfish and self-centered at times. In fact, it seems like the world sometimes applauds people who look out for themselves, no matter the cost to others. It can be hard to look outside of yourself to find ways that you can help others, especially when you feel like any effort you make may go unnoticed or unappreciated.

Yet in Philippians, Paul reminds us that we shouldn't do anything out of selfishness, but should find ways to value others more than we value ourselves. Maybe this looks like taking out the trash or helping your brother or sister with their homework. It's amazing how much better you will feel when you start to find ways to help others instead of just looking out for yourself. Even if people don't seem to notice what you've done, there is an inner peace and joy that comes from helping those in need because God made you that way.

God created you to have a heart that wants to serve and love others. God made us in his own image and that's the very heart of God. Ask God to open your eyes to places you can love and serve those around you. When you begin to focus more on others and helping those around you, you'll be surprised at what a difference a little bit of kindness and unselfishness can make in the lives of someone else and how much they appreciate it.

TAKEAWAY

Let go of selfishness. Look for ways to help those around you and to give your time and talents to benefit others.

WRITE ABOUT IT . . .

What are some ways you could be less selfish? Write down a few ways that you could immediately be more selfless and help others more in your day-to-day life.

DAY 52

Whoever claims to love God yet hates a brother
or sister is a liar. For whoever does not love
their brother and sister, whom they have seen,
cannot love God, whom they have not seen.

1 JOHN 4:20

This is a pretty strong verse that doesn't really mess around. It's basically calling you a liar if you claim to love God but hate another person. And the reality is, you probably have at least one person in your life who makes things difficult for you or is just hard to be around.

But you are called to look different than the rest of the world. The light of God should shine bright in you by loving those around you and finding joy no matter what may be happening in your life. That can be a heavy burden to bear at times, but there is also joy and peace when you choose to live your life the way God calls you to live it. When you choose to love those who are hard to love, you'll stand out from the crowd. It is hard to do that on your own, but God will give you the strength you need if you ask him.

The next time you find yourself in a situation with someone who irritates you or is just plain mean, remember that you are called to be different. And the nice thing is that loving people and responding to them with love becomes a habit and can make a huge difference in the lives of people around you every day. You are the light and love of God to everyone you meet and there's no better way to show that to others than responding with love to the very people who make your life difficult.

TAKEAWAY

You cannot hate a person and claim to love God. You need to respond to others with love.

WRITE ABOUT IT...

How can you show love to those around you?

DAY 53

May the God of hope fill you with all
joy and peace as you trust in him, so
that you may overflow with hope by
the power of the Holy Spirit.

ROMANS 15:13

Have you ever had something or someone in your life that you put all your hope and trust in and then you were disappointed? It's so easy to build people or things up in your mind and believe that if only those people would notice you, or if only you could achieve a certain goal, then you would be happy.

But there is a hole in your heart that only God can fill. That's why you may find yourself looking for all kinds of ways to fill yourself up, but still feel empty. God is the only true source of joy, hope, and peace in your life. When you realize how much he loves you and cares for you, then you can trust that he is always working out every detail of your life for good.

God knows that you struggle with feeling like there are things in this world that might bring you happiness. But he is always there waiting for you to bring your problems and worries to him so that he can fill you with joy and peace and you will overflow with hope.

 TAKEAWAY

God is the only source of true joy and peace, which allows you to have hope in your life in all circumstances.

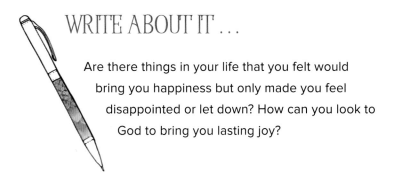 WRITE ABOUT IT . . .

Are there things in your life that you felt would bring you happiness but only made you feel disappointed or let down? How can you look to God to bring you lasting joy?

DAY 54 • ACTIVITY #9:
SUPPORT A CHARITY

Organize a lemonade stand or bake sale to support a favorite charity.

1. Invite a few friends to help you with the sale and ask an adult to help you.

2. Choose a charity or a ministry that you would like to support.

3. Make a couple of colorful signs advertising your sale and make sure you specify that all the money will go to charity.

4. Gather the supplies you'll need for the stand.
   * lemonade mix
   * several pitchers
   * cookies/brownies
   * paper cups and napkins
   * a box to put money in with change

5. Choose a busy spot to set up the stand.

6. Be polite and friendly and have fun!

DAY 55

But you, Lᴏʀᴅ, are a compassionate
and gracious God, slow to anger,
abounding in love and faithfulness.

PSALM 86:15

God loves you more than you could ever imagine. He loves you no matter what you have done or how much you have messed up. Sometimes it's easy to feel like you've disappointed everyone around you by choices you have made, but that's not how God loves you. He is slow to anger and is overflowing with love and faithfulness to you. That means that he is very patient with you and doesn't get angry every time you mess up. He loves you and is faithful to you no matter what you do or have done.

So when you make mistakes or feel like you've messed up too much to deserve God's love, remember that it's not possible to do that. Sometimes it can be tempting to put distance between yourself and God when you've done the wrong thing, but God wants you to run to him. He is always there waiting, full of love for you.

TAKEAWAY

God is slow to anger and loves you more than you can imagine.

WRITE ABOUT IT ...

What are some things in your life that you might do if you really let yourself feel how much you are loved? Are there some past hurts or disappointments you could let go of? New things you might try?

_____

_____

_____

_____

_____

_____

DAY 56

When they saw the courage of Peter and
John and realized that they were unschooled,
ordinary men, they were astonished and they
took note that these men had been with Jesus.

ACTS 4:13

Have you ever watched someone do something really brave and wished you had that same kind of courage? Sometimes when you see other people step out and take a chance on something, it can inspire you to do the same thing. There are so many things that can hold you back, like the fear of failure, getting hurt, or looking stupid. But then there are those amazing moments when you just decide to go for it anyway.

That's how Peter and John were as they shared about Jesus. There is no doubt that it was scary for them. They knew not everyone wanted to hear what they had to say. Yet these men felt so strongly about what they had experienced that they couldn't help but tell everyone about him, no matter what it might cost them.

And you know why they could do that? Because they had been with Jesus. It can be so hard to take a risk to tell others about Jesus or to share what he has done in your life, but when you spend time with him and experience what he can do, then you won't be able to keep it to yourself.

TAKEAWAY

When you spend time with Jesus, he gives you the courage you need to share about him and to let him guide you in your life.

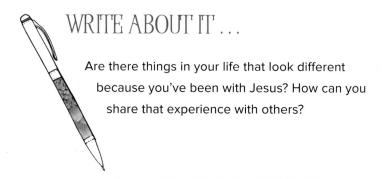

WRITE ABOUT IT . . .

Are there things in your life that look different because you've been with Jesus? How can you share that experience with others?

_____

_____

_____

_____

_____

_____

DAY 57

Jesus Christ is the same yesterday
and today and forever.

HEBREWS 13:8

Do you ever have times in your life when it feels like everything is changing? Just like the seasons change from fall to winter to spring to summer, life is always bringing new challenges and experiences.

Sometimes change is nice, but there are other times when change is really hard, like when friendships grow apart or your family moves to a new city. But the one thing that will never change is Jesus. He is the same yesterday, today, and forever.

No matter what else is going on in your life, you can count on God. He has been watching over your life since before you took your first breath. And he will continue to protect you and fight for you always. When the world around you seems uncertain or you feel afraid for what lies ahead, just take a deep breath and remember that God never changes. He will always be there, no matter what.

 TAKEAWAY

Jesus never changes. He is good and faithful.

WRITE ABOUT IT . . .

What are some things in your life that are changing
right now? Do you trust that Jesus will always
be the same in your life and help you through
whatever you might face?

"I have told you these things, so that in
me you may have peace. In this world
you will have trouble. But take heart!
I have overcome the world!"

JOHN 16:33

You have probably already figured out that sometimes life is hard. In fact, life is hard a lot of the time. There are times when you lose someone you love, a friend turns their back on you, or school is stressing you out and you aren't getting along with your parents. These things are all part of life.

God knows that life is hard. That's why he made a point to put it in the Bible. In this world you will have trouble. He didn't say "if", he said "you will". And when those hard times come, you can be sad, you can be mad, and you can be angry. It's okay to feel all those things because it's how you were made. It's also a good idea to talk to your parents or another adult you trust about the things you are struggling with in life.

The good news is God has overcome the world. Darkness doesn't have the final say in your life, God does. He is always working everything together for good, even when life is hard. Trust in him to take care of you and to heal your heart when it feels broken.

 TAKEAWAY

Life is hard, but God is always good.

WRITE ABOUT IT...

Does life seem hard right now? What are some things you are going through that you can let go of and trust God with?

Whatever you do, work at it with all your heart, as
working for the Lord, not for human masters . . .

COLOSSIANS 3:23

Work isn't always fun. Whether it's studying for a test
or helping with chores, those usually aren't the things
you love the most. It's much more fun to spend the day at the
movies or shopping with friends, but work is a necessary part
of life. Right now work probably doesn't look like a real job
like your mom or dad may have. For you, it might look like
being a good brother or sister, a good friend, working hard at
school, and practicing a sport or an instrument.

There are times when we feel tired and want to quit, but God
will give you the strength you need and has given you specific
gifts that you can use. Work hard to do well at whatever you
do, and the people around you will see that you are different,
and the difference in you is from God.

Remember that everything you do is for God. He has given
you your gifts and talents, your family, and your mind. He
has put you in your school and community because he knows
that you can make a difference in the lives of the people
around you there. As you study and do chores, remember that
you are doing it to bring glory to him and to let his light shine
in you.

TAKEAWAY

Work with all your heart because the things you are doing are for God.

WRITE ABOUT IT . . .

What are some of your daily responsibilities or chores? How would you do these differently if you keep in mind you are doing them for God?

_____

_____

_____

_____

_____

_____

RANDOM ACTS OF KINDNESS ROCKS

1. Go to a craft store or look around your neighborhood for good, smooth rocks.

2. Find some acrylic paints or paint pens.

3. Decorate rocks with words that remind you and others to be kind to those around you. Some examples are "Be Joyful!", "Be Kind", "Serve One Another", "Love Always".

4. Keep the rocks as a reminder to yourself or give them to a friend who may need encouragement.

So do not fear, for I am with you; do not
be dismayed, for I am your God. I will
strengthen you and help you; I will uphold
you with my righteous right hand.

ISAIAH 41:10

Not all fear is bad. Sometimes fear is your mind's way of protecting yourself from harm. It's why your parents probably taught you not to touch a hot stove or not to run out into the middle of a busy street without first looking both ways.

Then there are the fears that come from not trusting God with all the details of your life. It can be hard to surrender control and to take a leap of faith without knowing how it will turn out, but often that's exactly what God will call you to do. Fear whispers to you that you are alone and helpless.

The truth is that God is always with you. He will help you through any situation you face, no matter how scary or dangerous. He will give you the strength you need to get through it. So the next time you feel fear rising up in you, ask yourself who is bigger, the situation you are facing or God?

Replace your fear with prayer. Talk to God about what you are facing and trust that he will walk you through anything life brings your way, no matter how scary it may seem.

 TAKEAWAY

God will strengthen you and help you when you feel afraid.

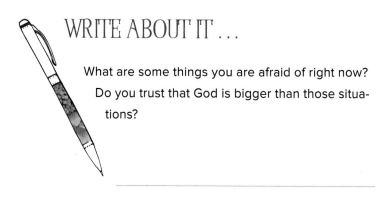 WRITE ABOUT IT . . .

What are some things you are afraid of right now? Do you trust that God is bigger than those situations?

Do everything without grumbling or arguing,
so that you may become blameless and pure,
"children of God without fault in a warped
and crooked generation." Then you will
shine among them like stars in the sky.

PHILIPPIANS 2:14–15

Do you do all your chores, homework, and everything else your parents ask you to do without arguing or complaining? It's hard not to complain or argue, especially when you feel like something is unfair or not what you want to do.

The apostle Paul wrote these words in the Bible and he had plenty to complain about. He was beaten and spent time in prison as he traveled around telling others about Jesus.

The thing about arguing and complaining is that it doesn't help you shine and you are called to shine in this world like the stars shine in the sky. The best way to do that is to go about your day-to-day life without grumbling about things. There are people who are closely listening to your words and watching your attitude, so think about whether or not you are making a good impression.

Everyone prefers to be around a person who is full of joy and encouragement, even when times are hard and things aren't really going the way you want them to go. You can choose to find joy. So look for ways to encourage those around you and to gladly do the things you are asked to do. And when you're tempted to complain, it may help to stop and remember things in your life that make you feel grateful.

TAKEAWAY

Don't argue or complain. You are called to shine.

WRITE ABOUT IT ...

Are there things or people in your life that you constantly complain about? How could you find ways to stop arguing and complaining?

DAY 63

It is for freedom that Christ has set us free.
Stand firm, then, and do not let yourselves
be burdened again by a yoke of slavery.

GALATIANS 5:1

When Paul wrote these words in Galatians it was because there were many people who were still trying to live under the original laws of the Old Testament. The Jewish people wanted the Gentiles to follow their rules, but Paul wanted the people to know that Christ set us free. Jesus died on the cross so that we could be free from our sins.

Sometimes it can be easy to forget the freedom we have in Christ. You may worry too much or feel afraid of what other people think about you. Sometimes you may even feel like you have disappointed God. But you have been set free from all those things through Jesus because he is the basis for all your security.

He came to heal the brokenhearted and set us free. That means that you can live your life worrying less about being perfect or doing everything right all the time. It means you don't have to live in fear of what others think about you because you are so loved by the God of the world. When you trust him, the chains that are holding you back from joy are broken. You are free from lies that you have believed about yourself and you can begin to see things from God's point of view. You realize that your life rests secure in Jesus because he has set you free.

 TAKEAWAY

God has set us free through Jesus dying on the cross. You are free to be exactly who God made you to be.

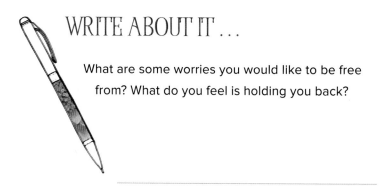 WRITE ABOUT IT ...

What are some worries you would like to be free from? What do you feel is holding you back?

DAY 64

Hold on to instruction, do not let it go;
guard it well, for it is your life. Do not set
foot on the path of the wicked or walk in
the way of evildoers. Avoid it, do not travel
on it, turn from it and go on your way.

PROVERBS 4:13–15

You probably have a habit of some kind. Maybe you bite your nails or pop your knuckles. Whatever it may be, habits are things we've done so often that we usually do it without thinking. Sometimes bad habits can be very hard to break because they become such a part of who you are.

The good news is that you can create good habits in your life. For example, listening to the people you trust and who love you, and doing the right things even when no one is watching. These kinds of habits might take time and discipline to develop. That's why Proverbs tells us to hold on to good instruction and guard it well.

The course of your life is determined by who you listen to, the habits you develop, and the people you surround yourself with. It's important to ask God to help you have wisdom in these areas so that you will be more likely to make good decisions and walk the best path for your life. The more you do it, the more it becomes the best habit you'll ever develop.

TAKEAWAY

Listen to good instruction in your life and make it a habit to follow it.

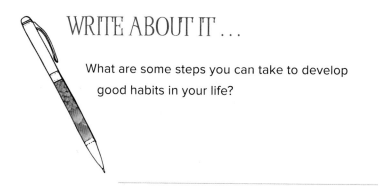

WRITE ABOUT IT...

What are some steps you can take to develop good habits in your life?

_____

_____

_____

_____

_____

_____

_____

DAY 65

Become wise by walking with the wise; hang
out with fools and watch your life fall to pieces.

PROVERBS 13:20 (THE MESSAGE)

Your friends make a difference in almost every decision you make. They are the people you spend the most time with and can influence your habits and how you act. That's why it is so important to choose to spend time with good friends who will help you make smart decisions. This means there may be people in your life who are fun to be around at times, but aren't necessarily the best ones to go to for advice about how to live or handle a tough situation.

Think about your friends. Are most of them good or bad influences in your life? Do they encourage you? Do they help you in your walk with God? Can you trust them? Or do they make you feel bad about yourself? Do they talk you into doing things you wouldn't normally do? Do they talk about you behind your back?

Make smart decisions when it comes to your friends. You want to spend time with people who will help you be a better person. If there's always a lot of drama and fighting, then ask God to bring you friends who will encourage you and support you. Those are the people who will build you up and make your life better.

TAKEAWAY

Choose good friends who are wise and will support and
encourage you.

WRITE ABOUT IT ...

Who are your closest friends? Do they give you
good advice? Do you trust them?

DAY 66 • ACTIVITY #11:
HOST A
MOVIE NIGHT

1. Ask your parents to find a good night on the calendar.

2. Invite a group of your friends to come over for a movie night; maybe have everyone wear their pajamas.

3. Pick a movie that's appropriate and that everyone will enjoy.

4. Order pizza, pop popcorn, and make a candy bar with different candy options.

5. Have fun being with your friends and remember how thankful you are to have them!

We have this hope as an anchor
for the soul, firm and secure.

HEBREWS 6:19

Life is sometimes like the ocean. It can be calm one day, but then rough the next. Have you ever been in a boat out in the ocean? The waves determine how the boat moves; there is no way for it to stay in one place without an anchor. Once an anchor is truly secured to the bottom of the ocean floor, the boat will stay in place no matter how windy or rough the sea may become.

Our lives can feel like a boat being tossed and turned, and we feel like we can't control what happens next or where we are going. But Hebrews tells us that Jesus is our hope; he is the anchor for our soul and will keep our lives firm and secure. We can get distracted and drift away from the things in our life that are most important, but Jesus's love secures us and helps us find peace.

If you are feeling overwhelmed by life, fix your thoughts on him and remember that the hope you have in his love and forgiveness is an anchor. He will hold you tight even when life gets hard and the waves seem like they are too much. He is your hope even in the darkest of times and worst of storms.

 TAKEAWAY

The hope you have in Jesus secures your heart and soul.

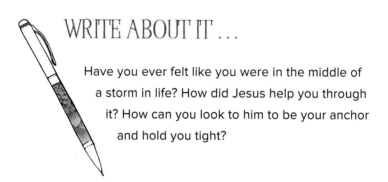 WRITE ABOUT IT...

Have you ever felt like you were in the middle of
a storm in life? How did Jesus help you through
it? How can you look to him to be your anchor
and hold you tight?

_____

_____

_____

_____

_____

_____

DAY 68

Why, Lord, do you stand far off? Why do
you hide yourself in times of trouble?

PSALM 10:1

Sometimes when we find ourselves in the middle of a tough
time, it's hard to understand what God is doing and why
things aren't going the way we wish they would. Have you
ever had a time when you've thought about asking God *why*?
Why he allowed this thing to happen or why he didn't change
a bad situation?

When you read through the book of Psalms, you will see
many times when the writers asked why bad things happened
or what God was doing. This doesn't mean that they doubted
the goodness of God. They just wanted to know why this
thing was happening to them.

God doesn't mind being asked why. His answer won't be
"Because I said so!" like your mom and dad may sometimes
say. He won't always give you an immediate answer and
often you won't know why things happened the way they did
until later on, if ever. But God wants to have a real relationship with you and that means it's okay to ask him to show
you where he is and why you are going through a hard time.
Talking to him and asking him questions will help you
remember how much he loves you even when life doesn't
seem fair.

TAKEAWAY

It's okay to ask God why something is happening in your life or to question how he is going to use a situation for good.

WRITE ABOUT IT . . .

What are some questions you have for God? Write about a time you didn't understand why something happened but it made sense later on.

Likewise, the tongue is a small part of the body,
but it makes great boasts. Consider what a
great forest is set on fire by a small spark.

JAMES 3:5

Anytime you open your mouth to say something, you should think about what you are about to say and ask yourself if it is true and if it is kind. You might be surprised by what you choose not to say when you think about those two questions first.

God knows that often we speak first and think later, which is why he reminds us that even though our tongue is a small part of our body, it holds a lot of power. In fact, Paul compares it to the way a small spark can start a huge forest fire. In the same way, it only takes one small word that is untrue or unkind to destroy a friendship.

Let's take the time to use our words carefully. Let's ensure that we aren't spreading gossip or saying something about a friend that we wouldn't say to their face. This will help you become a person that people trust because they know you are loyal, true, and kind. And those are the characteristics that honor God in our lives.

TAKEAWAY

Our tongue is powerful so we need to choose our words carefully.

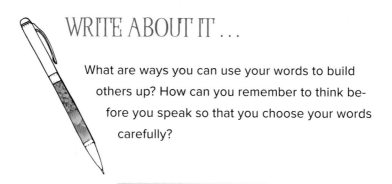

WRITE ABOUT IT...

What are ways you can use your words to build others up? How can you remember to think before you speak so that you choose your words carefully?

DAY 70

But he said to me, "My grace is sufficient
for you, for my power is made perfect in
weakness." Therefore, I will boast all the more
gladly about my weaknesses, so that Christ's
power may rest on me. That is why, for Christ's
sake, I delight in weaknesses, in insults, in
hardships, in persecutions, in difficulties.
For when I am weak, then I am strong.

2 CORINTHIANS 12:9–10

You may have already had a time in your life when you failed to achieve something that you really wanted. Failure can be hard to handle. It can cause us to feel pain and disappointment.

But sometimes failure can actually be positive. It often makes us stronger than we were before. Maybe you didn't get the grade you hoped for on a math test, but it helped you know how to be more prepared next time. Or maybe you didn't make the soccer team, but it helped you find a sport that you actually like better. Failure can help us find the gifts that God has given us.

Paul knew that God's power is made perfect in our weakness. There will be times in life when we fail, but God is stronger than our weaknesses and failures. If you let him, he will use those failures to make you strong and to lead you to the path he has for you. The next time you fail ask God what he wants you to learn then go where he leads you. Often an ending is really just a new beginning.

TAKEAWAY

It's in our weaknesses and failures that God can be our strength.

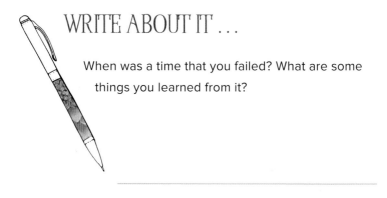

WRITE ABOUT IT...

When was a time that you failed? What are some things you learned from it?

Children, obey your parents in the Lord, for
this is right. "Honor your father and mother"—
which is the first commandment with a
promise—"so that it may go well with you and
that you may enjoy long life on the earth."

EPHESIANS 6:1–3

In case you haven't figured it out yet, your parents aren't
perfect. And although your parents might frustrate you
sometimes, God says we are to honor and obey our parents.
What does that look like?

It means that you should ask them for advice. Your parents
want what is best for you, and they can help you figure out
the best thing to do. They know your strengths and weaknesses so it makes sense to ask them for their opinion on
situations in your life. You should also pray for them and
encourage them. Your parents need your prayers, and it is nice
to let them know ways they have helped you and that you are
thankful for them.

And, most of all, you can honor them by telling them the
truth. It's hard to have a good relationship if you aren't honest
with them about what is going on in your life. You might be
surprised at how forgiving they will be when you decide to be
truthful, even when you've messed up.

Family relationships can often be hard. We have seen the worst side of each other but we must fight to honor God by honoring our parents. The way we treat our parents matters to God.

TAKEAWAY

It's important to honor God by honoring your parents.

WRITE ABOUT IT . . .

Do you let your parents know you appreciate what they do for you? What are some ways you can show them you love and respect them? How can you pray for them?

DAY 72 • ACTIVITY #12:
MAKE A
BUCKET LIST

A bucket list is a set of goals and dreams you have for yourself. It can help you figure out what is important to you and what you would like to achieve.

1. Get a piece of paper or write in a journal or notebook.

2. Make a few different lists of things. Here are some suggestions:
    *   Where would you like to travel?
    *   What would you like to achieve in school?
    *   What are some goals you have for extracurricular activities (dance, sports, band, etc.)?
    *   What are some ways you would like to take a risk or try something new?
    *   What are your dreams for yourself?

3. Keep the list in a safe place so you can look at it every now and then. Change it as you add new things and cross others off the list.

DAY 73

The LORD detests lying lips, but he delights
in people who are trustworthy.

PROVERBS 12:22

We have all told a lie at some point and it only takes one lie to make a person a liar. When you lie to people, they might lose their trust in you and trust can be hard to earn back once it's broken. The other problem is that one lie often leads to more lying. It can become easier and easier to not tell the truth as you work hard to cover up that you lied.

And while we like to think there are small lies and big lies, God hates all lying. It's much better to be real and honest because even though lies may make you feel good for a little bit, they eventually become a heavy weight to bear. Face the truth even when it is hard. It may lead to punishment, but at least you'll gain trust by being honest.

Ask God to give you the strength to be honest. He is always faithful and can give you the strength to do the right thing, even when it's hard.

TAKEAWAY

Lies will only destroy the trust people have in you. Tell the truth even when it is hard.

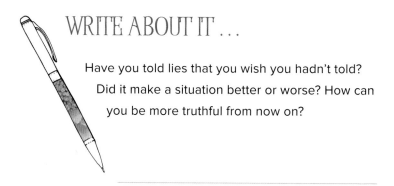

WRITE ABOUT IT . . .

Have you told lies that you wish you hadn't told? Did it make a situation better or worse? How can you be more truthful from now on?

DAY 74

Don't let anyone look down on you because you are young, but set an example for the believers in speech, in conduct, in love, in faith and in purity.

1 TIMOTHY 4:12

Paul spoke these words to Timothy as he started out his ministry and they are as important for you to hear today as they were for Timothy. It can be so easy to feel that you are too young to make a difference but God used many young people throughout the Bible to change the world.

David killed Goliath when he was just a teenager, Mary gave birth to Jesus when she was young, and it was a boy who shared his fishes and loaves with Jesus to feed 5,000 people. Don't ever let anyone tell you that you are too young to make a difference in the lives of others.

When you think about your life, what do you have that God can use? Are you good at sports? Are you a great student? Can you be a friend to someone who needs one? If you ask God to show you ways to make a difference in the lives around you, he will be faithful to do it.

God doesn't care about your age, he cares about your heart. You can set an example for people who are much older than you if you ask God to help you live faithfully for him. Don't ever let people underestimate you based on your age.

TAKEAWAY

You are able to make a difference in the world no matter how young you may be.

WRITE ABOUT IT . . .

Are there things you feel like you can't do until you're older? What are some ways you can let God use you right now?

_____

_____

_____

_____

_____

_____

DAY 75

For whoever has will be given more, and they
will have an abundance. Whoever does not have,
even what they have will be taken from them.

MATTHEW 25:29

Each one of us has been given specific gifts. Whether you play sports or an instrument or dance or are a great student, you have been given that ability by God. When we put those gifts to use according to God's purpose, great things can happen in our lives and the lives of others.

God is the one who is the giver of all good gifts. No matter what your gifts are, God gave them to you for a reason and a purpose. Are you using the gifts and talents God has given you? There are things inside of you that God uniquely gave you and you will feel his joy when you use those to bring glory to him. God has put some version of that inside of every one of us. There is something inside you that will help you feel how much God loves you.

We're all part of the body of Christ and every part matters. There is no part of your life or your gifts that is insignificant. You were created to love and serve God, no matter what else you do in life. When you use your abilities for God, he will bless your efforts and continue to help you find ways to make a difference. Be faithful to use your gifts to show others what God has done in your life. That's the best way you can demonstrate how grateful you are that God made you in such a unique way.

TAKEAWAY

God has given you specific gifts and talents. When you use them, he will continue to bless you with more.

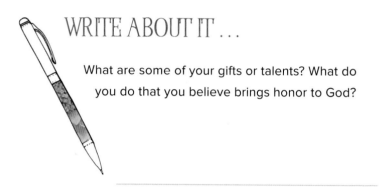

WRITE ABOUT IT...

What are some of your gifts or talents? What do you do that you believe brings honor to God?

For we are to God the aroma of Christ among
those who are being saved and those who
are perishing. To the one we are the smell of
death; to the other, the fragrance of life.

2 CORINTHIANS 2: 15–16

Our sense of smell is a powerful thing. It can bring back memories, make someone clear a room, or fill you with a sense of calm and happiness. And it's interesting that Paul refers to us as being the aroma of Christ to both believers and non-believers. Through our words and actions, we are the fragrance of Christ's love to those around us. That is a huge privilege and responsibility. It means that we need to show love to others, follow where Christ leads, and do our best to make sure that we're not putting out any aroma that will cause people to be turned off by Christ.

When you live a life that honors God, people will look at your life and sense that there is something different about you. They'll want more of it in their own life because they can see how it has given peace and joy even in difficult times. The sweet smell of God's grace that has been poured out in our lives should be so powerful that it draws others in. That's better than any fragrance you can buy in a store because it's real and it will last forever!

TAKEAWAY

You are the fragrance of life and peace to those around you.

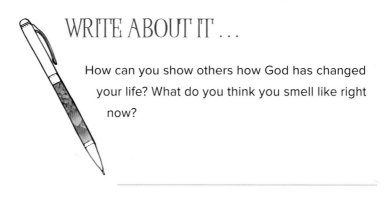

WRITE ABOUT IT ...

How can you show others how God has changed
your life? What do you think you smell like right
now?

And Elisha prayed, "Open his eyes, Lord, so that he may see." Then the Lord opened the servant's eyes, and he looked and saw the hills full of horses and chariots of fire all around Elisha.

2 KINGS 6:17

In 2 Kings 6, Israel was at war with the nation of Aram. God would tell the prophet, Elisha, what Aram's next move would be and so Israel defeated Aram over and over again. But then the king of Aram found out that God was using Elisha to defeat him and so he sent an army to attack him. Elisha and his servant woke up one morning to find that they were surrounded by an army! Elisha's servant panicked because it looked like certain defeat. But Elisha prayed and asked God to open the eyes of his servant so he could see what was truly happening. All of a sudden, the servant could see that there was an army of angels surrounding and protecting them from the attack.

We've all had times in our lives when it feels like we are constantly in battle. It can be fighting against our own mind and the fears that creep in during the middle of the night or it can be situations that come up with friends or family members. We can start to feel like we're all alone and there is no way we can possibly win the fight. This is when we usually panic. But we have the maker of the universe fighting for us and angels protecting us at all times. We just need to ask God to open our eyes so that we can see all that is on our side and remember that God is constantly protecting us and fighting for us.

TAKEAWAY

God is always fighting for us and he has an army of angels on his side.

WRITE ABOUT IT . . .

What are some hard situations you are facing right now? How can you trust God to help you fight these battles? Ask him to open your eyes to see him working for you.

DAY 78 • ACTIVITY #13:
COMMUNITY SERVICE PROJECT

>>>>>>∞··—·—··>

There are so many ways that you can serve your community or your school. Ask a teacher or a parent for suggestions on a project that you and your friends can do to give back and let your light shine. This could be serving meals at a homeless shelter, volunteering in a Sunday School class, or gathering clothing or food donations for a local charity.

> Jesus said to her, "Mary." She turned
> toward him and cried out in Aramaic,
> "Rabboni!" (which means "Teacher").
>
> JOHN 20:16

There are probably people in your life who call you on the phone and as soon as you hear their voice, you know exactly who is on the other end of the line. Their voices are as familiar to you as your own and you would know them anywhere.

After Jesus had been crucified, Mary Magdalene went to the tomb and saw that the stone had been moved. Mary Magdalene stayed outside the tomb crying until two angels appeared to her and said, "Woman, why are you crying?" She responded, "They have taken my Lord away." At this point, Jesus was standing there but she didn't recognize him. She thought he was a gardener, so she said, "Sir, if you have carried him away, tell me where you have put him and I will get him." Then Jesus said to her, "Mary."

As soon as he spoke her name, she knew him instantly. Knowing someone merely by the sound of their voice shows how close you are to that person and how often you talk to them. It's a sign of a real relationship.

Do we recognize God's voice when he talks to us? Because

that's the kind of relationship he wants to have with you, the kind that when he whispers your name you know immediately you are in the company of your Savior.

TAKEAWAY

God wants us to have a deep relationship with him so we know when he is speaking to us.

WRITE ABOUT IT...

Spend some time talking with God. What are some ways or things you can do to make that relationship stronger?

_____

_____

_____

_____

DAY 80

If we are thrown into the blazing furnace, the
God we serve is able to deliver us from it, and
he will deliver us from Your Majesty's hand.
But even if he does not, we want you to know,
Your Majesty, that we will not serve your gods
or worship the image of gold you have set up.

DANIEL 3:17–18

Shadrach, Meshach, and Abednego were in an impossible
situation. They either had to bow down before the king
or choose to honor God, and they knew if they didn't choose
the king it would mean death. They chose God, were thrown
into the fiery furnace, and had no idea if God would save
them from certain death. That's what it looks like to truly
put your faith in him 100%. It's easy when life is going along
as planned, but what about when the "even if he does not"
moments come? Do you trust him in those?

There will be times in your life when God doesn't do what
you wanted or hoped for and it's hard to understand. But God
is always working every situation out for the best. Our faith
will be strengthened when we trust him even during the times
we don't understand him.

Ultimately, God did save Shadrach, Meshach, and Abednego
from the flames, and the king himself was able to see the full

power of God because of their strong faith. This is what it means to have fearless faith that can change the world. Ask God to help you have this kind of faith in your life.

TAKEAWAY

We need to learn to trust in God's goodness even when he doesn't do the things we hoped.

WRITE ABOUT IT...

Can you remember a time when you felt disappointed in the way God handled a situation? Can you see how it turned out to be a good thing even though it was hard then?

_____

_____

_____

_____

I'll refresh tired bodies; I'll restore tired souls.

JEREMIAH 31: 25 (THE MESSAGE)

You know how you feel at the end of the school year? Summer is so close that you can smell the sunscreen you will slather on before you head to the pool for the rest of the day. It's like you can see the finish line but you're so tired that you have no idea how you're going to make it there. You still have projects to finish and tests to take and all you really want to do is take a nap and then maybe watch some television.

We all reach points in our life when we're worn out, but life still goes on. God understands that life can wear us down. He made us to need rest, which is why it is healthy to get at least eight hours of sleep every night. We function better, we think more clearly, and it improves our moods. But often it's not just our physical bodies that need rest, it's our souls. The physical things can wear us down, but it can be the mental and spiritual battles that feel like they're going to kill us. And that's why rest doesn't just mean sleep. It can mean taking a break from your phone, scheduling some time to hang out with your friends, or reading a good book.

God never meant for us to walk through these things alone or without promising to refresh our tired soul. He knows that life is hard so we can go to him and ask him to help us find rest when we feel like we can't go on.

TAKEAWAY

God refreshes our tired body and soul.

WRITE ABOUT IT . . .

Do you feel tired right now? What are some ways
you can rest and let God refresh you and give
you strength?

_____

_____

_____

_____

_____

_____

> She (Hagar) gave this name to the LORD
> who spoke to her: "You are the God
> who sees me," for she said, "I have
> now seen the One who sees me."
>
> GENESIS 16:13

The story of Hagar begins when God promises Abram an heir, but his wife, Sarai, has yet to get pregnant. So Sarai has her maidservant, Hagar, conceive a child with her husband. Sarai becomes jealous of Hagar and mistreats her, causing Hagar to run away with her son, Ishmael.

Hagar feels that all hope is gone when, suddenly, an angel shows up and helps her. Hagar knew that God hadn't forgotten her and so she gave God the name El Roi, which means the God Who Sees. She is the only person in the entire Bible to give God a name.

Hagar was a minor character in the story of Abraham, yet in God's eyes she was no less important. He saw her. He provided for her.

We can often feel our lives are small when we think about all that God deals with every day. Do the details of our life really matter? But Hagar's story is a reminder that we serve El Roi—the God Who Sees. He sees all the small details of our lives. He sees who we are, who we hope to be, and who we can become. He meets us in the deserts of our life and promises to give us everything we need.

TAKEAWAY

God sees all the small details of your life and cares about them.

WRITE ABOUT IT ...

What are the things in your life that are important to you but may seem small to other people? Do you believe God cares about these things?

DAY 83

'For I was hungry and you gave me nothing to
eat, I was thirsty and you gave me nothing to
drink, I was a stranger and you did not invite
me in, I needed clothes and you did not clothe
me, I was sick and in prison and you did not
look after me.' "They also will answer, 'Lord,
when did we see you hungry or thirsty or a
stranger or needing clothes or sick or in prison,
and did not help you?'" He will reply, 'Truly I
tell you, whatever you did not do for one of
the least of these, you did not do for me.'

MATTHEW 25: 42–45

Every day there are people around you who are in need of
something. It can be a basic need like food or clothing or
it could be an emotional need like love and acceptance. Every
one of us needs help sometimes and you can ask God to show
you the people around you who have a need.

We are supposed to love our neighbor like we love ourselves,
and when we help those in need it's the same as if we are
doing it for Jesus himself. When he talks about the "least of
these" he doesn't mean those people are less than, but that
they are the ones who are forgotten or looked down upon.

When you come across someone in your community who is in need, look for ways to show them the love of Jesus. It's the most visible way we can show Jesus to the world around us.

TAKEAWAY

When we help those in need, it's the same as helping God and showing his love to the world.

WRITE ABOUT IT . . .

What are some ways you can help someone in need? Where can you serve in your school, church, or neighborhood?

DAY 84 • ACTIVITY #14:
BLESSING BAGS

This is a bag that is full of essential items and some snacks that you can easily keep in your parents' car and hand out when you see someone in need.

1. Buy a box of gallon-size plastic zipper bags or save grocery sacks and use those.

2. Ask your mom or dad to take you to the store and buy things to put in the bags. Here's a list of suggestions:
   • Toothbrushes
   • Toothpaste
   • Shampoo (travel sizes are great)
   • Conditioner
   • Lip balm
   • Deodorant
   • Granola bars
   • Cheese or peanut butter crackers
   • Fruit snacks
   • Bottled water
   • Socks

3. Assemble the bags and keep them in a larger bag or box in your car so you will have them ready when you see someone who may need one.

DAY 85

Two are better than one, because they have a
good return for their labor: If either of them falls
down, one can help the other up. But pity anyone
who falls and has no one to help them up.

ECCLESIASTES 4:9–10

Life is better when you share it with a good friend. There is
something about a friend that makes the hard times easier
to bear and the good times even more fun. God knew that
we weren't meant to live life all by ourselves and so he gave us
hearts that want to love others. But sometimes friendship is
hard. Maybe you've been hurt by a friend. Or maybe you've
just had a difficult time making good friends that you can
trust. But don't underestimate the importance of friendship
and what it can mean in your life.

We all need friends who love us and help us when we are having a hard time. We need friends to encourage us, defend us,
and to give us strength. We have to take the risk of being hurt
because it's worth it to love and be loved by a good friend.

The best friendships are the ones in which you share a faith in
Jesus. Those are the friends who truly understand your heart
and your priorities. Those are the friends that will encourage
you to keep chasing after God and to make him first in your
life. These are the friendships that will go the distance and
make you both better people.

TAKEAWAY

We need friends to make life better.

WRITE ABOUT IT ...

Who are your closest friends? How do they encourage you? How can you encourage them?

Let us not become weary in doing
good, for at the proper time we will
reap a harvest if we do not give up.

GALATIANS 6:9

Have you ever felt like you are tired of doing good and trying so hard? Does it seem like sometimes your efforts go unnoticed and no one appreciates how hard you are working? Here's what you need to know: DON'T GIVE UP.

Don't let the enemy discourage you or tell you that what you are doing doesn't matter. Your effort matters. You matter. God sees you and he sees your heart even if it feels like no one else does. Keep going and looking for ways to change the world around you. Don't quit being kind, working hard, and loving the people in your life.

The thing about a harvest is that it takes time to develop. Seeds are planted and watered and the sun shines bright, but often we can't see all the fruit that will grow until much later. Goodness and kindness can be like that. But God promises that you will see a harvest when you keep going.

TAKEAWAY

Don't give up or quit doing the good things in your life.

WRITE ABOUT IT ...

Have you felt discouraged? Can you look back and see a harvest from some good things you have done?

DAY 87

This is the day that the LORD has made;
We will rejoice and be glad in it.

PSALM 118:24 (NKJV)

The world seems a little chaotic and scary sometimes. There is bad news everywhere you turn and it can feel like there is nowhere to find joy. It can be easy to worry about what tomorrow will look like and to focus on all the tragedy.

But God wants you to find joy even in the middle of the sadness. Today is the day the Lord has made no matter what else is going on. Sometimes just taking the time to be thankful for what you have can help you find joy. You woke up this morning with breath in your lungs and with a God who loves you more than you can even comprehend. You have another day to make a difference in the world and so let's choose to rejoice and be glad in it.

All the wrong in the world isn't going to go away. But when you choose to fight for joy you will find it even in the middle of the dark. God made this day and he would have made this day even if it was just for you. Find a way to rejoice and be glad in it.

TAKEAWAY

Every day is a gift we've been given from God.

WRITE ABOUT IT...

How can you fight to find joy even when life is
hard? How can you show God that you are
thankful for this day you've been given?

_____

_____

_____

_____

_____

_____

DAY 88

As iron sharpens iron, so one
person sharpens another.

PROVERBS 27:17

Iron is shaped by heat and pressure. It takes both of those things to mold it and make it into what it is supposed to be. Have you ever seen a wrought iron gate or fence? It took a lot of work to form it and to get all the edges and curves just right.

And just like iron is sharpened and shaped, we are shaped by the people around us. God uses our parents, our friends, and our teachers to form us and make us better than we would be without their influence in our life. That's why it's so important to choose good friends.

There will be times when a good friend may have to tell you that you're not on the right path or maybe *you* have to say those words to a friend. That can be part of the heat and pressure of iron sharpening iron. But in the end, the process is worth it. You will make each other stronger and better people than you would be otherwise. Don't be afraid to talk to a friend if you see them making bad choices. Pray that you would have people in your life that would do the same for you.

TAKEAWAY

Friends sharpen each other like iron and make each other stronger.

WRITE ABOUT IT . . .

When was a time when you had to have a hard conversation with a friend? Was it worth it? Would you want a friend to talk to you if they saw you making bad decisions?

On the last and greatest day of the festival,
Jesus stood and said in a loud voice, "Let anyone
who is thirsty come to me and drink. Whoever
believes in me, as Scripture has said, rivers
of living water will flow from within them."

JOHN 7:37–38

If you are an athlete or have ever done anything outside in the heat, you may know that staying hydrated is key to success. You have to hydrate before you play and that means you have to start drinking plenty of water at least twenty-four hours ahead of game time.

The thing about hydration is you have to stay on top of it if you want to be at your peak performance level at game time. Once you realize you're not hydrated enough and start to cramp, it's too late. Your body can't really make up for it, no matter how much you drink. You have to be prepared.

Your relationship with Christ is a lot like being hydrated for a game. You need to be in daily communication with him through reading your Bible and praying. When we are full of God's love, we are living our life at peak performance. When we let ourselves get depleted and a hard time hits, we can feel scared and tired. Jesus is our living water. He is the only thing that can fill us up and give us the strength we need to get through life.

TAKEAWAY

Jesus is the living water and the only thing that fills us up.

WRITE ABOUT IT . . .

What are some ways that spending time with Jesus refreshes you and makes you stronger?

DAY 90 • ACTIVITY #15:
TASTE TESTING

>>>>>>>>——•••———•———•———•••——>

This is a fun way to see how unique you and your friends are and that what one person thinks is best isn't necessarily the way others think!

1. Ask your parents to find a good time on the calendar and invite a few friends over. This activity will probably be easiest and most fun with a small group of 3–4 friends.

2. Decide what items you want to taste test. Make sure to find out if your friends have any food allergies or sensitivities ahead of time. Here are some ideas:
   - Two different brands of ice cream
   - Different kinds of chocolate bars
   - Two different kinds of fruit (Example—an orange vs. a pineapple or different kinds of apples)
   - Different kinds of soft drinks
   - Different kinds of potato chips or crackers

3. Set up various stations and hide labels under each plate, bowl, or cup where your friends can't see them.

4. Write down the results for each friend and compare who liked what and the reasons why.

5. Have fun and laugh at how differently we are all created and how unique our taste buds are.

DAY 91

In their hearts humans plan their course,
but the LORD establishes their steps.

PROVERBS 16:9

You are moving into the years where you are going to have so many decisions to make, and it is crucial for you to have your own personal relationship with God. What do you want to be when you grow up? What are your hopes and dreams? You don't have to know the answers to these things, but it's good to start thinking about them.

Reading your Bible and praying are important so that you can learn how to hear the voice of God. There will come a time in your life when you will have to make choices that affect your future, and God can help guide you. You might wonder if God wants you to do something that doesn't feel like something you would typically want to do, for example.

We've all been there. We love making plans, but sometimes God has something different in mind for us. But the times that we are willing to let go of our own plan and surrender to his? He will never do us wrong.

You can make your plans and have your hopes and dreams, but God knows us even better than we know ourselves. So hold onto your plans with a loose hand and be flexible to God's voice. He knows the ways you can make a difference, the things that will truly make you happy, and what you need before you even know you need it.

TAKEAWAY

God will direct our paths and guide us into what is best for us.

WRITE ABOUT IT ...

What are some of your plans? Will you trust God enough to hold them loosely and let him guide you in the right direction?

_____

_____

_____

_____

DAY 92

Godly sorrow brings repentance that
leads to salvation and leaves no regret,
but worldly sorrow brings death.

2 CORINTHIANS 7:10

Lately, we are seeing a lot of powerful people whose lives have been ruined by their bad choices. We see them facing consequences but we might wonder if these people really feel sorry for their mistakes.

These words in 2 Corinthians sum it up best, when we have done something wrong and created a mess, do we experience Godly sorrow or worldly sorrow?

God knows we are going to mess things up. Humans have been messing up his plans and turning their backs on him since the beginning. It's in our nature. Sometimes it's just easier to grab what we think we want instead of waiting for what God has for us.

God never wants us to choose the sorrow of the world that leads to death. And not only can we turn back to him, he will fix what we have broken because that's how much he loves us. God is always pursuing us, no matter how much we've messed things up. He will never—not even one time—give up on us; God wants us to live in a way that we run to meet him when we see him, no matter how far away we've been.

 TAKEAWAY

God loves us no matter how much we mess up. We only have to ask for forgiveness.

 WRITE ABOUT IT . . .

Is there a mistake you've made or a time when you felt sorry for what you did? Can you trust God with that and know that he loves you no matter what?

Blessed are the pure in heart,
for they will see God.

MATTHEW 5:8

There will be times that you face a decision and try to discern what God is calling you to do. Sometimes there isn't a good option and bad option as much as just trying to figure out which way might be a little better than the other. Sometimes we get it right and sometimes we don't.

But here's the great thing about God and what Matthew 5:8 promises us, "Blessed are the pure in heart, for they will see God." It doesn't say, "Blessed are those who never screw up" or "Blessed are those who do all the right things" because God is always more focused on our hearts than on our actions. We are flawed people just trying to do our best and sometimes we fall short.

If we allow ourselves to fall in love with Jesus completely and totally, we'll find more and more that our heart is always in the right place. That's when we experience the pure joy of walking in the way God has planned for us. Our desires start to line up more and more with God's desires.

But that doesn't mean we become perfect. God isn't worried about us being perfect; he knows exactly what we are with all our flaws and weaknesses. He's our creator and knows what to do with our shortcomings. When our hearts are pure, then we can really be the person God made us to be.

 TAKEAWAY

God wants us to have a pure heart that seeks him.

 WRITE ABOUT IT ...

Have you ever had a time when you thought you
were doing the right thing and it didn't turn out?
Was your heart in the right place?

_____

_____

_____

_____

_____

_____

And I will be to her a wall of fire all
around, declares the LORD, and I
will be the glory in her midst.

ZECHARIAH 2:5

The world tells us we have to do it all, be it all, and achieve it all. We need to do big and important things. You need to make good grades, be a good athlete, and be involved in a million extracurricular activities. Your generation has never worked harder to make sure that you measure up and worried so much that you don't.

But can you trust God to give you what you need? Deep down, everyone struggles with believing God is going to lead us to what is best for us. What could happen if you begin to live in a way that you quit building walls around yourself and let others see who you really are? What if you lived in a way where you really believed God promises to be a wall of fire around your life and the glory in your midst?

God wants to make your life so big that walls can't contain it. He wants you to have peace and contentment. He will be your protection. He will be the wall of fire all around you and remind you that your life is enough because he is enough.

TAKEAWAY

God has built a wall of fire around you and he will let his light shine in your life.

WRITE ABOUT IT ...

What are some ways you feel pressured to be more or do more? Do you believe that God will give you all you need?

_____

_____

_____

_____

_____

_____

Jesus looked at him and loved him. "One thing you lack," he said. "Go, sell everything you have and give to the poor, and you will have treasure in heaven. Then come, follow me." At this the man's face fell. He went away sad, because he had great wealth.

MARK 10:21–22

This wealthy young man runs to Jesus, falls to his knees, and is excited to learn more about his teachings. Jesus lists off the commandments and the man proudly says that he has kept all of them. But Jesus looks past the surface and tells him he will have to sell everything he has and give it to the poor. The young man decides almost instantly that this is a step too far and walks away sad.

Sometimes, as much as we love God, we are limited by holding on to things he has asked us to give up. God wants to bring new friendships, relationships, and opportunities to serve him but we hold on to our fears, and our safety nets because we don't really believe that God is going to give us everything we need, when the reality is that he is going to give us so much more. It's times like this that we need to have a fearless faith.

How different would that man's life have looked if he had said yes? How different would our lives look if we say yes?

 TAKEAWAY

Jesus will always give us so much more in return than anything he asks us to give up.

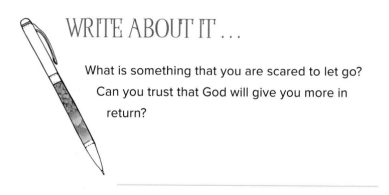 WRITE ABOUT IT . . .

What is something that you are scared to let go? Can you trust that God will give you more in return?

_____

_____

_____

_____

_____

_____

DAY 96 • ACTIVITY #16:
ENCOURAGING NOTECARDS

>>>>>>>————∞∞————•———•———•••———→

Now that we are down to the last activity and final week of this devotional, go back through and find some of the verses or words that meant the most to you. Write them down on notecards. You can decorate them and make them pretty if you want to! Then keep them in your backpack or in your room to give out to friends when they are in need of some encouragement or love. You could also stick them in their school locker or lunchbox as a fun surprise!

But the Israelites went through the sea on dry ground, with a wall of water on their right and on their left. That day the LORD saved Israel from the hands of the Egyptians, and Israel saw the Egyptians lying dead on the shore. And when the Israelites saw the mighty hand of the LORD displayed against the Egyptians, the people feared the LORD and put their trust in him and in Moses his servant.

EXODUS 14: 29–31

There have probably been times in your life when a situation looked so impossible that you can relate to the Israelites. There isn't a choice that looks safe. It's those times when it is easy to let fear and doubt overwhelm us. How many times have we thought, "That's impossible!" or "There is NO WAY that situation can be fixed!"?

When tough times come, we tend to trust in what we can see and forget what we believe. Essentially, people have always been the same, and the children of Israel were no different. They wondered why God didn't just leave them in Egypt to die instead of bringing them out to the desert. Sometimes we lose sight of the God we serve because we are blinded by the fears and problems right in front of us and they become all we can see.

But we serve a God who is going to give us what we need,

exactly when we need it. He parts the seas just in time, he stills the storms just when it's about to overtake us, and he makes the path smooth even if it seems impossibly rough. He's just waiting for us to trust him.

TAKEAWAY

The God who parted the Red Seas for the Israelites is the same God we serve today. He can do the impossible in any situation.

WRITE ABOUT IT . . .

What's a problem you are facing that seems too big? Will you trust God to help you through it?

DAY 98

But the angel said to her, "Do not be afraid,
Mary; you have found favor with God. You will
conceive and give birth to a son, and you are
to call him Jesus. He will be great and will be
called the Son of the Most High. The Lord God
will give him the throne of his father David,
and he will reign over Jacob's descendants
forever; his kingdom will never end."

LUKE 1:30–33

Think about Mary and how she probably wasn't much older than you when the angel dropped this bombshell. As far as we know, she didn't ask for this role in God's plans. God simply showed up in her life and she became part of his plan. He saw something in her heart and her spirit and knew she would be faithful.

When God calls us to that unbelievable thing or hard place, do we trust him? Do we have hearts that are open to go where he leads no matter the cost? Can we say the words of a young Mary who simply said, "I am the Lord's servant"? There are so many times in the Bible when we see God speak to much older and experienced people who pushed back with all the reasons they couldn't do what he was asking. And yet here is Mary, who doesn't ask a single question other than to wonder how this could happen.

It's also a great reminder that we don't have to stress out over what God is calling us to do; he will show up and lead us where he wants us to go. We just have to have a heart that's willing to follow him where he leads.

TAKEAWAY

God can use you no matter how young you are when you have a heart that will follow where he leads.

WRITE ABOUT IT . . .

Will you go where God leads you in life even when it doesn't make sense? Can you ask him to make you brave like Mary?

_____

_____

_____

For as high as the heavens are above the
earth, so great is his love for those who fear
him; as far as the east is from the west, so far
has he removed our transgressions from us.

PSALM 103:11–12

We are almost to the end of our time together and here's
what you need to know, maybe most of all. God's love
for you is so great and so big and so unconditional. He sees
the real you and thinks every single part of you is wonderful.
You are exactly what he had in mind before he ever laid the
foundations of the earth.

Jesus died for your sins on a cross because he loves you so
much. If you had been the only person on earth, he still
would have done that just to save you. And so when you think
of the cross, think about how one beam goes up and down to
remind you how high God's love is for you. The other beam
goes from east to west, which can remind you that's how far
he removes our sins.

There is nothing you can't do, can't achieve, or can't accomplish
because God is always with you. He will give you strength
when you are weak. He'll make you brave when you are scared.
He'll come running to meet you when you mess up. Live your
life in a way that shows the world you know you have a father
who adores you. Be strong, be brave, be kind. You are loved.

TAKEAWAY

God loves you as high as the heavens and has removed all your sins. You are free to love and live.

WRITE ABOUT IT . . .

Spend some time writing down what God's love means to you and what that means for your life. Will you be more willing to take risks and live life in fearless faith and knowing that you are so loved by the creator of the universe?

_____

_____

_____

_____

_____

_____

For if you remain silent at this time, relief and
deliverance for the Jews will arise from another
place, but you and your father's family will
perish. And who knows but that you have come
to your royal position for such a time as this?

ESTHER 4:14

Here's the thing about God. He often uses the most unlikely people to get things done. Look at the story of Esther. One brave girl in the right place at the right time saved an entire nation from being destroyed. One brave girl who wasn't afraid to speak up changed the course of history.

There is no doubt that God has placed you where you are, in this time and in this generation, for such a time as this. There are people all around you who are in desperate need of God's love and grace. We live in a world that needs fearless people to speak out on the difference between God's truth and the lies that this world will try to sell you. Can that feel scary? Absolutely. But is it worth it? Always.

The story of Esther is a reminder that God uses unlikely, ordinary people all the time and you aren't the exception to the rule. He is a God who specializes in using ordinary, daily acts of faithfulness to change the world around us. We only have to be willing. We only have to have fearless faith.

TAKEAWAY

When we are willing to be brave, God can use your life to make a huge difference in the world.

WRITE ABOUT IT . . .

What are you afraid of? How can you trust God and live life fearlessly?

MELANIE SHANKLE

Melanie Shankle is the *New York Times* Bestselling author of *Sparkly Green Earrings*, *The Antelope in the Living Room*, and *Nobody's Cuter Than You*. She is also the author of *The Church of Small Things* and *Everyday Holy*. She speaks at nationwide events and writes daily on her blog, Big Mama. Melanie is a graduate of Texas A&M University and lives in San Antonio, Texas with her husband, Perry, and daughter, Caroline.

@melanieshankle

Melanie Shankle

@BigMama

www.thebigmamablog.com

ABOUT THE ARTIST
HEATHER GAUTHIER

Heather Gauthier lives with her husband and two little boys in San Antonio, Texas. From her small home studio, which doubles as a LEGO cave, she produces over 100 original paintings a year. After years of living everywhere from Chicago to South Africa, she finally settled into a career of full-time painting in her home state of Texas. Her style is a culmination of her experience working with textiles and flowers, and countless hours of staring at animals on the internet.

 @heathergauthierart

[f] Heather Gauthier Art

www.HeatherGauthier.com

Connect with Faithgirlz!

http://www.faithgirlz.com/

www.facebook.com/Faithgirlz/

www.instagram.com/zonderkidz_faithgirlz/

DEVOTIONS FOR WOMEN FROM

Melanie Shankle

EVERYDAY HOLY

FINDING A BIG GOD
IN THE LITTLE MOMENTS

100 DEVOTIONS

100 DEVOTIONS FOR
FINDING A BIG GOD
IN THE LITTLE MOMENTS

ZONDERVAN®
.com

**AVAILABLE EVERYWHERE
BOOKS ARE SOLD.**